Advance Praise

"I highly recommend this book whether you are a business owner or not—because it is really a book about making time for more personal fulfillment in your life. Who doesn't need more of that?"

—Amy Rose, LCSW

"Glitter, Duct Tape, and Magic *is a fun, quick read that reminds me of so many of the reasons I'm in business for myself and why I love serving my clients. As a coach to many "busy" entrepreneurs, I know that many will not take the time to read much of the self-help work that's available, but this book is filled with bite-sized morsels that make it easy to read, absorb, and put in practice the tactics that can help us all be more focused, productive, and fulfilled as professionals. Filled with timeless wisdom, proven strategies, and a heavy dose of reality checks, all mixed in with humor and heart,* Glitter, Duct Tape, and Magic *is a must-read for busy women who have realized that it's time to create their own definition of "having it all" and are looking for a guidebook to help them do just that!"*

—Angi Bell
Inspire Results Coaching

"This book combines everything Michelle Spalding is good at: educating you on practical methods to grow your business and teaching you the importance of applying spiritual principles to ensure you enjoy the ride. Michelle's honest, generous, and caring approach displayed on each page and shared with great vulnerability will save you from making many of the same mistakes she made in the beginning of her entrepreneurial journey. If you want to learn how to love your business instead of regret it, this book is for you. A must-read for entrepreneurs wanting more."

—Rhonda Ryder
Author of *Delicious Alignment: How 25 Women Learned to Love and Transform Their Bodies Using Abraham-Hicks and the Law of Attraction*

*To my soul sisters in business:
may you always have all the
success your hearts desire.*

Glitter, Duct Tape, and Magic

Glitter, Duct Tape, and Magic

BY MICHELLE SPALDING

Happy Zinnia Publishing
Un-Settling Books
Boulder, Colorado USA

Cover Design and Typography: Sally Wright Day
Editing: Maggie McReynolds
Author's photo courtesy of Meghan Vail Photography.

ISBN: 978-1-7347146-0-9

Contents

Foreword

By Regena Garrepy
ESSENCE LEADERSHIP GUIDE + COACH MENTOR

There are two things that have deeply impacted my evolution as a human: becoming a parent, and being an entrepreneur.

Taking on these two roles was like signing up for a rigorous personal development bootcamp. Not for the faint of heart! I happen to take them on only a year apart. Talk about feeling like you know nothing. Prior to having my son, I had been a schoolteacher. I thought I knew kids, but it turns out that when it comes to your own child, it's a completely new world. The same was true for being an entrepreneur. I knew nothing about launches, products, sales, marketing, or even a profit and loss statement.

Through the past fifteen years, I've experienced some

of life's greatest challenges and most significant rewards. I've come face to face with self-doubt, perfectionism, fear, mistakes, indecision, and the desire to hide. Yet working through each of these challenges has brought me more strength, fulfillment, freedom, and love than I could have imagined. I have lived the dream of building a business from my passion, working from home to be there for my son, developing my leadership, traveling the world, speaking on stages, and making more money than I could have thought possible my first year of teaching fourth grade.

While being a parent has ripped my heart out and kept me up at night, I have never once doubted my decision to be a parent. Not true of being an entrepreneur. For years, I've had a running joke with my best friend about quitting our businesses and working at a certain well-known bookstore—at least, until the bookstores started disappearing. Scan the articles on the dark side of entrepreneurship and you'll find that business owners feel more stress, depression, and loneliness than those who work for others.

And yet more than half of Americans want to be their own boss. They want the dream of flexibility, freedom, and the potential to create and grow their idea into a successful, thriving, company. That's all possible. But being your own boss isn't *easier* than having one.

As I read through the pages of *Glitter, Duct Tape, and Magic,* I found myself nodding in resonance with Michelle's stories of entrepreneurialism. So much emotional turmoil and hours could have been saved if this book had existed when I was struggling to build and define my business.

Besides coaching women and running retreats and women's circles, I also serve as the Director of Training for author and speaker Mike Dooley. He writes the Notes from the Universe and was featured in *The Secret*. It was through our Infinite Possibilities Trainer conference and subsequent local monthly meetings that I got to know Michelle.

As magic would have it, I showed up to a meeting feeling burned out and exhausted. I was grateful that we had a guest speaker that day because I wasn't up to inspiring anyone. When Michelle began talking, I felt she was speaking directly to me that day. By the end of her talk, I had experienced a huge lightbulb moment. What I had felt were weaknesses that I had to overcome were opportunities to up-level my business by hiring virtual support. The intimidating aspects of where and how had dissolved, and I felt clear (see Chapters Twelve and Thirteen!). In the next two years, I more than doubled my income and finally broke the six-figure mark.

Over the past six years, I've also had the honor and opportunity to mentor Michelle through her participation in my group mastermind and coaching programs. I've watched Michelle persevere and develop herself to pour that level of personal leadership into her business. I am amazed at what she's built and inspired by how she's made it. She chooses to meet each challenge with the intention of becoming better, not bitter.

And I've pushed Michelle. I've asked her to do hard

things, uncomfortable things, in order to break through personal upper limits. And she did them. I invited her to look at parts of herself she didn't want to face, to accept and love herself more, to step more fully into her power as a woman and a leader and a voice for others. Every time I asked her to rise, she did.

Each chapter of *Glitter, Duct Tape, and Magic* is filled with her personal stories of courageous vulnerability along with real tools and exercises that are the equivalent of a Disney Fastpass for the wisdom she's acquired. Just like this book, she embodies both the practical and the magical. She brings a little bit of mystical to the mundane. This book will remind you that you aren't alone, and that whatever struggle you're facing right now, there is something in this book that can help. Michelle walks her talk, and she'll walk with you.

I often joke with her that she creates and achieves more in a month than anyone I know. It's true. When Michelle has a vision, she puts her heart, brilliance, and integrity behind it. She's learned to trust her intuition and show up to lead her business with strong boundaries and a kind, passionate heart. She is a conscious leader who cares about contributing to the well-being of humanity and the Earth. We need more leaders like Michelle.

Grab a journal, pen, and highlighter. Write down the applicable wisdom and reclaim the essence of your business through the inquiry questions she asks at the end of each chapter.

Introduction

Is your business supporting you in living the life you want to live? Maybe it's a path you pursued hoping it would get you where you want to go, and now you're not sure you like it there.

I'm sure you're smart, talented, and working hard. You may even have clients and customers who sing your praises. So why does it feel like something's off?

You're not alone. Many of us start a business to escape from a situation we find less than satisfying. We want something better for ourselves, even our world, and we believe we can achieve that through entrepreneurship. It's only later that we find ourselves frustrated, exhausted, and, often, further from our dreams than we were before starting a business.

We live in a time where people are hungry for authenticity. Yet we often try to be someone other than who we truly are in our work.

I propose that we stop leaving our souls at the door when we walk into the office. That we stop trying to do it all, and start doing the things we love. That we learn to listen to signs, trust our intuition, and take inspired action while weeding out the hype.

In the pages that follow, you won't find me pretending to know it all; far from it. I'll share with you some mistakes I've made so that, hopefully, you won't make them as well. You can learn from my example, rather than go down the path I took to figure it out. I'll also be sharing with you many of the resources that have helped me. I want you to know that I'm just like you: a person who wants the most out of life. I even hope to make you laugh a little as I share with you some stories of my entrepreneurial adventures.

I'll give you many examples of taking action—intentional, focused action, not action for the sake of being busy or looking productive to others. You won't find me advising you to do a bunch of things and see what sticks— just thinking of that wears me out. I'm talking about action that you feel inspired or guided to take.

Since you're reading this book, you've doubtless heard of the movie *The Secret*. When that came out fifteen years or so ago, I wrote myself a big fat check, posted it on the wall next to my newly created vision board in my office, and impatiently waited for everything I wanted (and needed) to come my way. I was in a deep financial mess, and at the same time, I hated the work I was doing. A new vision sounded great to me.

But guess what? None of the things on my board came to me. Not because I wasn't wishing for it and hadn't created a beautiful vision of what I wanted, but because I hadn't considered how I wanted to feel. I learned, over time, that inspired action—action in alignment with how I wish to feel in my life and my work—is what takes me to my destination. After all, just because the car is moving doesn't mean you're going in the right direction.

Knowing what action to take requires getting clear on your soul's calling: what you'd like your life to look like, who you wish to serve, how you want your life and business to feel, and then checking in with all that often as you navigate your days and the decisions you make. I'll share with you my thoughts on that, and more.

Speaking of your soul's calling, or purpose, let's set the record straight here. Most of us make this much harder than it has to be. I've met people who tell me they aren't sure what their soul is calling them to do or how to find their purpose. After a few questions I use with clients to guide them to their answer, they generally say something like, "Wow, I never thought of that being my calling. Is that big enough?"

Whatever makes you smile and makes you feel happy is your soul's calling, and it's absolutely big enough. For some of us, it's a business. For others, it's rescuing animals, or working toward a more peaceful world. There are over seven billion people on the Earth, which means there are over seven billion different ways for any one person to express their soul's calling. Don't compare your calling to mine or anyone else's. Yours is special, and only *you* can do it.

I'm a Business Alchemist. I don't change discarded

aluminum cans into gold. But I do help people transform their business obstacles and challenges into a way of life that works for them. This is what I want for you. I don't know all your answers. I can't, because you do. In my private client work, that's exactly what I help people figure out: how to dig deep and find their own right answers. So you can see this alchemy in action, I'll share my stories and those of some of my clients in the pages ahead (I've changed client names to respect their privacy).

Lastly, you'll find many suggested exercises in this book designed to help you individualize the information and make it work for you. It's up to you if you skip them or do them. I've found that when I read books with the intention of simply getting to the end of them, I don't get the shift I was hoping for. But when I actually follow along and do the exercises that accompany the books I read— BAM! New doors open. I'm hoping you won't skip these exercises just for the sake of finishing the book.

Now let's go and make some magic together.

CHAPTER ONE

Girl Gets Wild Idea and Opens a Business

*Our fear of the unknown and our fear of making
mistakes trick us into focusing on what we don't
know or can't do. When we give ourselves
the freedom to be uncertain and less than
perfect, then we can start thinking, 'What
do I know? What can I do?' That's when the
adventure starts—earning, thriving, conquering,
failing, recouping, and having a ton of fun.*

—KRISTIN SMITH

Once upon a time, there was a woman who wanted to make a difference in the world through the work she did.

She wanted to have a clean home, well-behaved children, a home-cooked meal on the table each day at 6 pm, stylish hair, a strong and lean body, and the time and resources to take a family vacation more than once every few years.

She dreamed of volunteering in her community, making a local impact, and being of service to those in need. When her kids were young, she also envisioned helping on school field trips and volunteering in their classrooms.

She knew her life was out of control. She was tired, weary, and nearly on the verge of a complete breakdown. Her work as a real estate paralegal had her working over 60 hours a week, leaving little time for her family, let alone fun. Between her job and her commute, she found her kiddos were spending more time in the care of others than they did with her.

Her health was suffering as well. At thirty-four years old, she was having chest pain. After she wore a heart monitor for a week and underwent more tests than it took to get her through high school, her doctor told her that her physical symptoms were a result of stress. And if she wanted to feel better, she'd need to change how stressful her life was.

She wanted to reclaim her life. So she decided to start a business where she thought she could make an impact with her work, as well as have freedom, flexibility, and all the things she desired. She hired someone to create a logo, wrote a business plan, built a website, and bought the software she'd need. Then, a few months later, she turned in her notice.

She did it! In October of 2005, she opened her virtual doors and started the real estate consulting and coordinating business that would transform her life. Her business was a new concept in Florida: providing transaction coordination services to real estate agents and helping them provide great service to their clients while making the most of their time.

Oh, the lessons she would learn along the way! It turned out she didn't even know what she needed to know yet. She created a nice website, provided a great service, and spent money on marketing and advertising to get the word out. And some of it worked, at least enough to garner her first paying client.

She worked hard for this client. Her work caught the eyes of the title agent in the transaction, and that led to an introduction to a big office. That introduction turned out to be just what every new business needs: a foot in the door at a place in need of her skills.

That introduction came with the request that she come and present at one of their weekly sales meetings. To say it went badly was an understatement. She bombed. But, thankfully, there was someone in attendance who knew that she had something valuable to bring to his office in spite of her lack of presentation skills. Her passion for her work and the services she was providing shone brightly, and she was able to pick up a few more paying clients.

Within a few months of opening her doors, she was introduced to a few other offices who all needed her services, which led to even more clients. Things were going great, she thought. It was like any new relationship or adventure—in the beginning, it was fun and felt almost magical. Until it wasn't.

As time went on, she grew weary. In order to reach her goals, she pushed, she hustled, and she worked insane hours. She kept telling herself that "one day all of this will pay off," and that she would finally have the life she wanted. Having no formal training in business or entrepreneurism, she simply did what was modeled for her in the places where she'd worked before.

When her health began to suffer yet again, she didn't make the connection to stress. After all, her symptoms were different than they had been when she was a paralegal. Instead, she simply felt weary and doubted her ability to be an entrepreneur. More than once, she told a friend she wished for an easier life. She even joked about taking a job flipping burgers. At least when you left your shift, you didn't have to take your work home with you.

She was exhausted, frustrated, and ready to call it quits when she found a mentor she trusted who asked her some detailed questions about her dreams, her vision, and what she expected of herself. It was with her mentor's help that she realized she was doing no one any good trying to do it all—least of all herself. She learned that in order to make the impact she truly wanted and to help others, she would have to say yes to doing things differently. She might even have to stop doing some things altogether.

Her challenges didn't magically transform that day. No Prince Charming showed up with a glass slipper or swooped her off to his castle. This was real life, not a fairy tale. But she embarked upon a journey to look at her relationship with time, the way she did her work, and what she valued most in her life. And while the journey continues (as it will never really end in her lifetime), she now has more free time, energy, and joy in her life. Her health is better, and her work is impacting even more people than she ever envisioned back when she started out.

From Fairytale to Reality

Where we leave off in her story, we pick up in the stories of many who are just like her. While this story is obviously about me, it's also one that most women business owners I've met can intimately relate to. I have a feeling that it could also be your story. Perhaps, like me, you were wanting freedom and flexibility in your life. You wanted to provide a service or product you're passionate about, so you, too, have started a business. But now you find yourself out there working very hard, and trying to create something you love and are proud of is leaving you frustrated and exhausted. It doesn't have to be this way. You can feel the way you want in your life and business while providing a service or product you're passionate about.

Over the years, I've discovered that some days in business are sparkly like glitter, some days are held together thanks to duct tape, and on other days, we know we are where we are because of something magical (some call it God) that we can't truly define. I believe that there is also something magical out there we can tap into if we choose. I hope that as you read this book, you'll see that too.

Speaking of what you call it, let me tell you a story about my friend Helen. One day while we were talking, the topic of spirituality came up. Helen instantly tensed up and told me she doesn't believe in God. I asked her why. She said her family had forced her as a young child to attend a Pentecostal church after her mother's death. In that church, Helen was taught that God was a force she must please. She must act a certain way and follow rules she didn't feel were right for her.

I asked Helen if she believed there was a force or energy that connected us all and that she could call on for support and guidance.

Yes, she said.

I asked her if this source was loving and kind.

Yes, she said. I asked her what she called it.

She said, "energy," or, "energetic higher source."

I told her that what she described was what I called God, and that I didn't think if we called it Purple it would matter. What did matter is that we called on it, that we believed in it and that we let it guide us.

So, for the sake of this book, I'll mix up the language I use. You'll find the words Higher Source, God, Divine, and maybe even Purple. You can substitute the word you use if you like. Whatever we call it, it's all a bit of the magic that we can access anytime we wish.

In the pages that follow, I'll be sharing some ideas to help your business and life sparkle. I'll show you that even when you're not where you wish to be, you can get there if you can get clear about what you want to feel.

I hope to help give you the courage to proudly rock that duct tape holding things together, knowing that you have the power to transform any obstacles in your way. And I'll help you bring in some magic from the Universe, which will give you the clarity and support to know

exactly which step is the next right one for you in living
the life you desire.

CHAPTER TWO

When You Can't Stand Your Boss— and You're the Boss

Expect the unexpected, and whenever possible, BE the unexpected.

—LYNDA BARRY

*I*t was all going well, and then it wasn't. I was just a few years into running my own business and felt like I hated just about everything about it. Most of all, I hated myself. After all, I was the one who had made this mess. And, unlike having a job working for someone else, I wasn't in a place where I could just quit my gig and find another one. I had a team, a lease, and financial obligations up the wazoo.

To outside observers, I was successful, and, on paper, mostly profitable. I'd gone from being a solopreneur and doing everything to having a small team working from a commercial office we leased. I'd done something many people told me I couldn't do. But I wasn't happy. In fact, I was miserable inside while trying to hold it all together, fearful of what others would think if they found out my secret.

How was this possible? How could I have started a business, leaving a workplace that was taking a toll on my health and family, only to end up in a place where I wasn't sure I liked what I'd created or the person I'd become?

I was my own boss, something I'd dreamed of and worked hard to make happen. Yet, there I was, at the point where I didn't like my boss anymore. There, I said it! I didn't like my boss. What the hell was wrong with me? I wondered this more times than I could count.

After years of working to help other entrepreneurs, I know now that I wasn't alone. But at the time, I sure felt like a crazy woman. I was terrified to admit how awful I felt about where I was in my life.

You too?

None of us do what we do as entrepreneurs because we're looking to torture ourselves. I think we all genuinely believe that we have something that will help others, and we want to share it with the world. In all the books I've read, and there have been hundreds, most leave out the part about resenting the very thing you've created. Instead, these experts are sharing with readers the shiny, happy parts. The implication is that if you're not feeling that way, then there are easy action steps you need to make that happen—and here they are!

Barf.

Truth be told, I thought there was something wrong with me. Looking back now, I can see how silly that was. But I can also say that I sure wish I'd known then what I know now about personal development and spirituality. Boy, the heartache and aggravation I could have avoided. But I was too busy working and fretting about how to fix things to stop and analyze what was happening in my life or how I was feeling.

Wrestling Imposter Syndrome

Having a business that appeared to be "working" while feeling like a failure sure made me feel broken or that I'd done something wrong. I knew that something was missing, but I thought it was about getting more business and the need to be bigger. I didn't know then that it was something deeper and more personal. Looking back, I realized that I'd missed an important part I didn't even know about. I'll share more on that later in the book.

My anger and frustration didn't come up overnight. It happened slowly. Before I realized it, I was in an unhappy place.

I remember reading that if you put a frog in a pot of lukewarm water and then turn on the heat under it, he won't notice. He'll sit there and adjust until it's too late. But if a frog is put into boiling water, he'll jump out instantly to try to save himself.

I hope no one has ever actually tested this analogy, but it's been told and retold to make a point. I truly felt like that frog, like I was in a pot of boiling water and it was too late for me. I was miserable, resentful, and, worst of all, angry at myself for not knowing how I'd gotten there or even what to do about it. I felt like the villain one moment and the heroine the next—each day felt like a fight to see who would win. This constant battle wasn't playing out on a big screen or in the pages of a book, but in my life. While I hope you've never experienced this feeling in your business, I want you to know that it's okay if you have. Sometimes figuring out what you want comes from seeing clearly what you don't.

When I share this analogy with people, I can almost see a light bulb turn on over their heads. They, too, feel like the frog who started off in cool water and now finds the heat unbearable. And with that, they realize they can now take the leap, and begin to make the changes needed to save themselves and their business.

Whose Fault Is It, Anyway?

Initially, I blamed my frustration on others. I think that's a default many of us are wired with a survival instinct of a sort. That's certainly where it started for me.

There were certainly challenges that did involve others. And at first, *they* felt like what was wrong.

I hired Molly to work part-time just before moving into the new office space. She was a neighbor and mother to one of my children's friends, and her resume led me to believe she would be a great fit. On top of her skills, she was bilingual, and many of our clients loved that she could speak Spanish. Looking back, I see the mistakes I made here—especially hiring someone I hadn't vetted properly. But, in the moment, Molly felt like the solution to my problem.

At first, I was so swamped by the logistics of the move and running a business that I chose to ignore many of the red flags. Molly's time sheet didn't match the actual hours she worked, and often included a few more hours than we'd initially agreed upon. Tasks she'd been assigned went undone without explanation. She had a certain eagerness to search the internet for just the right place to order lunch for the office, using my credit card, and didn't have that same enthusiasm for the actual work she was hired to do.

Oh, the lies I told myself to keep Molly on staff. I thought I was helping her by giving her the benefit of the doubt. I thought I was training her, and that, eventually, she'd get it. I was training her, alright; I was teaching her to take advantage of me. I was just too close to it at the time to realize it. But I knew deep down in my heart that Molly wasn't working out.

Only later did I realize something: I'd kept Molly on because I didn't want to be wrong about hiring her. And I didn't want to fire the mother of my son's friend. I thought I was being a "good boss," but I wasn't. I was simply allowing someone to take advantage of me.

It's funny how we'll keep people in our lives who we know aren't treating us with the respect and kindness we deserve, simply because we don't want to upset them. We spend so much time fretting about being seen as mean for asking what we want, and for settling for less than equal respect. Gosh, I suppose this could even be the makings of another book. For now, know that it's okay to ask for what you want, and to settle for nothing less.

I beat myself up for this one for a very long time. I put helping Molly above what was best for me and my company, only to cause harm to myself. But like that little frog I told you about earlier, I didn't see it at the time.

Eventually I fired Molly. She filed a grievance with the state claiming she was wrongfully terminated. Thankfully, I had documentation of the many incidents that led to letting her go. I won. The problem was, I'd already done the damage to myself.

I began to feel that I wasn't a good boss, and I wasn't a good entrepreneur, either. On the outside, I looked like I had it all together. I think we women are great at this type of charade. I smiled with the clients and laughed with my team. I did all the things a mom was supposed to do. I was going through the motions and, at the same time, hiding how awful I felt. Funny, I'm not sure that even in the moment, I could have told you what was wrong, other than that I felt lost, confused, and completely alone.

Of course, I wasn't alone, certainly not in feeling as I did. Several years later, while on a sales call with a real estate agent, I asked the agent why she was seeking my company's services. She said, "Because I hate my business and I hate myself."

Instantly, I could feel her intense pain. She went on to explain that she'd done everything her sales coach had told her to do, and it had worked—her income was the highest it had ever been. But she was about ready to close it all down and walk away. Between tears, she told me that her children and grandchildren lived in another state, and she'd flown them all in to stay at a nearby resort for a family vacation. They were in town for six days, but she was so busy with her business that she'd had only a handful of hours on a few of the days they were there to visit.

It broke my heart to hear her story. I listened and let her cry for quite some time. Then she shifted and seemed embarrassed she'd just cried to a stranger. She apologized, telling me she had no idea why she'd brought it up. I assured her that she was safe and that I was glad I was able to hold space for her to release that. I also let her know she wasn't alone and that I, too, had been there, looking like I had it all together and being the success others looked up to, but totally hating the business. And I told her it was okay to cry.

Back when I was in the throes of hating myself and my business, I kept asking, over and over, "How could this have happened? Where did I do wrong? What did I miss? Wasn't this what I worked hard for?" I thought that having a business and being free of the restrictions of being an employee would make me feel great. Sadly, I was beginning to have chest pain again and I wasn't sure I could keep this up much longer. I even recall thinking, maybe my former boss was right: maybe this won't work.

Little did I know that the Universe was conspiring to help me and that, just like magic, a door was about to reveal itself that I could choose to walk through.

Perhaps like me, you, too, are in a place where you're not happy with your business and your life. At this moment, I'd say, just breathe and hang on tightly to that hope you had when you started on your entrepreneurial journey. I'm not going to lie to you and tell you that if you do my "five easy steps," it will all change. But I will say to you that if you want things to change, they will. Be kind to yourself. Trust the magic. Keep an eye out for the doors that lead to where you want to go.

CHAPTER THREE

Whose Version of Success Are You Working Toward?

If you don't like the road you're walking,
start paving another one.

–DOLLY PARTON

I t was clear that something had to change. I was exhausted, angry, and on the verge of calling it quits.

I had more self-doubt than a middle schooler going through puberty looking for a date to the school dance. I was short with my children, the very ones I wanted to spend more time with when I started my business. I was disturbingly angry at random strangers in traffic. More than a few times, I was ashamed to find myself snapping at customer service reps on the phone.

I began going to networking events and workshops, reading books, and doing everything I could think of. This meant I was gone a few nights a week and occasionally on weekends, which was not what I wanted. But I'd convinced myself that one day it would all come together, and I'd finally have some freedom.

The thing about all this "one day" stuff is that we're never promised another day. And while I agree that goals are important, so is feeling how we want to feel in life, which, for me, was feeling free. I wanted to have freedom and flexibility in my life. At that point, they felt like foreign concepts.

Just about every business book or guru's workshop teaches you how to grow your business. Make it bigger, make more sales, sign more clients. More, more, more. I believed all of it. When I wasn't working in the business or attending an event, I was busy trying to implement everything I learned to grow my business because that's what the experts were teaching me I needed to be successful.

What I really wanted wasn't more. I wanted better. I didn't know what "success" even meant to me, and yet it was something I was chasing, hoping that when I achieved it, everything would feel better.

Note: It's critical that you clearly define what success looks like to you. Otherwise, you're likely to look for something you'll never find.

The bigger my business grew, the more sales we had, the more frustrated I became with what I'd created. How could this be? I loved the services we provided, the people I worked with, and most of the clients we served.

One evening, while working late at the office, I broke down and began to cry, which then turned into a sob. My sobbing continued for what felt like eternity, and I was grateful to be alone in my office. Being a rather private person, I know I would have never done this at home where my children could have seen me, or if my team had been around. I couldn't recall the last time I'd cried like that. It felt good to get it out. I think I went through an entire box of tissues in the process.

After crying my eyes out, I began to laugh. I just started laughing. I don't even recall if there was anything in particular I was laughing about, I was just laughing out loud. At this point, I began to wonder if this was what a nervous breakdown looked like: crying uncontrollably one moment, then laughing out loud the next. Rather than Google if these were, in fact, symptoms of losing my marbles, I shrugged it off and just sat there for a moment, thinking about what had just happened.

Instinctively, I picked up a pen and a yellow legal pad of paper and began to scribble a list of all the things I didn't like about my business and my personal life. This list included the hours I was working, the time away from my children, the employee who was draining my energy as well as my finances, the clients who were difficult to work with, and my health.

The Secret About The Secret

It was many months before I wrote this massive list that I'd watched *The Secret*, a viral movie at the time. The teachings of that movie and book are very simple: what we focus on we attract—in other words, the Law of Attraction. It further posits that our thoughts are power-ful, and if we change the things we think about, our lives will change. If there are things we don't like, we shouldn't give them our attention. That what we resist, persists, so we should simply focus on what we want. At least, that was my understanding of the material being taught at that time.

My instincts were telling me something different. They were telling me that I needed to make a list of what was troubling me, what was making me frustrated, and what I knew had to change. While making this list, I didn't stop for one moment to think of how I would transform any of it. I simply scribbled on one sheet of paper after another after another until I was pretty sure I'd written down everything I had inside me. Feeling complete, I read the list out loud.

Making that list and reading it aloud helped me articulate what was making me unhappy. I had no immediate solution to any of it, but I was beginning to feel hopeful. For the first time, I had some clarity. I'd opened space to create a vision to transform some of my biggest challenges.

One of the biggest things I wanted to change was my work environment. I missed being there when the kids came home from school. They often hung out at my office, but that wasn't what I wanted for them and me. On top of that, the office suite next to ours was filled with a particularly rowdy bunch. I'm still not sure exactly what they did, but there was a lot of cheering and celebrating throughout the day, which we found distracting. Several of them smoked and chose to do so outside of my window while chatting it up and sitting on the ledge.

Once, I knocked on my window and put my finger

over my lips to show them the universal sign of shush—and was flipped off. It was another clear sign that this was not the place for me or my team. Yet here I was, about five months into a two-year lease. I had no idea how to get out of it.

A few weeks later, I was reading a book as part of continuing education training for my real estate broker's license, a task I'm required to do every two years to keep my license active and in good standing in the state of Florida. I came upon a chapter describing the elements of a commercial lease. I read that the lease not only needed to state the term, which in my case was twenty-four months, but that it must also state the total amount due for that duration and reflect that in monthly payment terms. In other words, my rent was $2,000 a month, so the lease needed to show a total due of $48,000 payable in monthly installments of $2,000 on or before a certain date.

In reading the workbook, I realized that a lease without this statement was legally considered a month-to-month arrangement. My lease didn't have it. I couldn't be held accountable for the total financial amount due for the full two years! And so I could get out of the lease without any financial repercussions.

I put it out to the Universe that I wanted to change my work environment, and something magical happened. The exact information I needed, to solve the problem I clearly announced I needed help solving, was presented to me, nice and neat. If I hadn't made that list and gotten clear on what I wanted to change, I might not have connected the dots between my lease and the workbook. I would have missed the sign that was there to help me change something I desperately wanted to.

Interestingly, I've repeated this same course in the years that have followed. But I've never seen any reference to leases in it since. I guess I only needed it that one time.

Before I got honest with myself and created the list of things that weren't working for my business and life, I was focused on something that felt more like an escape than a personal reckoning. I'm not saying we can't or shouldn't look ahead and dream about a new car, a new home, or whatever we'd like. But I am saying that dreams alone weren't moving me forward. Sure, I might have manifested the new house, the new car, or the new whatever, but I would have still been dealing with an office space that was taking me away from my family. The list I created helped me gain clarity about what was most important to me at that time—and that was so much deeper than a fancy new toy.

Just seeing that there was a way out of the office environment that wasn't working for me, I began to feel a little more hopeful and relieved. Now I just had to figure out, with 2007 technology, how to manage a team remotely.

Brave New World

I called a team meeting a few days later and explained the situation. I told everyone how working in an office was making me feel, about how magically a solution had appeared, and that I wanted us all to work from home.

We all had a long talk, and I asked for feedback and input about how we'd make this a success.

What were their fears and concerns about this new arrangement? Were they willing to try it? How did they think our clients would react? What could I do to help support them in this transition? Everyone was on board with the idea. Best of all, they were willing to do whatever it took. After all, having no commute and the option to work in their PJs sounded like a dream come true to everybody.

Soon, our lease was terminated, the suite was vacated, and my team and I were navigating the new waters of working from home while still feeling like we were a real business. In early 2005, when I started my business, working remotely was a new concept in my industry. Many of the professionals who supported real estate agents worked side-by-side in the same office with them. We'd already proven we could work apart from our clients successfully by being in a different office building and still delivering great service. Now we needed to find a way to create a united front as a company while being miles apart from each other, and in an industry that was still not entirely on board with the remote working concept.

It all happened very quickly, as things to do when they are meant to be. Each thing that needed to happen to make it work just seemed to appear. There was magic happening in ways I couldn't have imagined, magic that would take me to places I'd never even thought of. Many of the things that came about were direct solutions to the things I wanted to change on my list.

This was a powerful exercise, and one that I've done again over the years, mostly without the sobbing that took place that day. The idea to make a list came to me at a time when I was in a dark and frustrating place. And while the answers didn't appear instantly, there was relief in writing down the situations I didn't like, then releasing them to a Higher Source to help me solve.

Getting clarity around how you want to feel and why feels curiously missing from some of the teachings from the Law of Attraction—at least, as it was presented to me at the time. I didn't care about a new home, a new car, a sparkly watch, or a designer purse—things I was supposed to want to have. While I wouldn't have turned any of them down, they weren't really that important to me. What was important to me was so much more, but in order to know that, I had to step back from the things outside myself and reconnect with what was meaningful to me. I had to identify where I'd taken a wrong turn and drifted away from what mattered to me most.

When I began coaching, I brought this exercise into my practice. As a result, I've witnessed powerful results in the lives and businesses of my clients. Below are the steps I recommend you follow, should you, too, feel that the work you're doing isn't bringing you the joy you wish for.

Your Turn: An Exercise

Find a quiet space where you won't be interrupted. If you can go to a park, or someplace else in nature, that's ideal, but not necessary. I find that sitting outside with my bare feet on the Earth helps ground me, but if it's

January in Chicago, there will be no unnecessary time outside for this girl.

To ground your energy inside, I recommend you find a comfy place to sit. With your feet planted firmly on the floor in front of you, take a few deep breaths to connect to your body. As you are taking those deep breaths, put your hand on your heart and set the intention to connect with the Earth below you.

Pick your favorite pen and a pad of paper. You'll likely end up needing more than you think, so a pad is ideal. Once you have your tools together, start thinking about the things you've been fretting about in your mind. Make a list of all the things that you're not happy with.

Write down anything that you don't think is working, the things that frustrate you, the things that anger you, the things you'd like to see changed. Don't hold back. This is your list, and you don't have to filter it for anyone. Write until you think you've written everything possible. Remember, you're not writing about how you'll solve these issues, or about who you'll go to for help, or even about what a solution would look like.

Once you have your list, I recommend you say a prayer to whomever you pray to ask for support, guidance, and wisdom around solving all the things you've listed in a way this is for your highest good. Ask that obstacles be removed, doors revealed, and people identified who could assist you.

This is where the magic happens. Now that you've listed the things you'd like to see change, shared that with the Universe, and prayed for support, you'll start to see a shift happen. Not likely that moment, but it's entirely possible! Just be open to signs, like the example I gave earlier about my lease. Doors are about to appear before you. You've simply got to open them when they do.

CHAPTER FOUR

Honey, You'd Better Change Your Thinking

Your thoughts and beliefs have a far more significant impact on the success of your business than any marketing or advertising.
—MICHELLE SPALDING

I'd solved a huge issue by moving my business from a brick-and-mortar office to a virtual one. But there were still significant obstacles between me and the true freedom I envisioned for myself.

My sister had recently died in a car accident, and my family was not only grieving but we were also working to help create a new, healthy life for her toddler daughter. My relationship with my then-husband was continuing to unravel, which meant zero support from him in my business; his work schedule was his priority. The real estate market was beginning to slow. Things were so bad in our industry that a woman I met at a party, after hearing I was in real estate, said, "I'm sorry."

I could go on for hours listing the many challenges, disappointments, and troubling situations that were happening inside and outside my home. But that's not going to help you or me. The point is that I, like most of us, had a lot going on. All those things were real; they were happening. But, as a friend once told me, "You can't control what happens, you can only control your reaction to it." In an out-of-control time in my life, it became clear that I could control one thing: me.

Affirmations

My thoughts needed a significant overhaul, and so I began a long journey, which continues today, of personal and spiritual development. One of the first things I started using were affirmations.

In the beginning, I used affirmations purely to help my business grow—remember, I thought growing my business was my problem back then. I started with things like, "I am a successful businesswoman who loves her work." Yup, that was a huge stretch. I felt about as far away from my concept of success as I could be, and I didn't love what I did for work even a little. At first, I cringed each time I said it, especially when I did it in the mirror as suggested. It felt like I was telling myself a lie. After all, I had proof it wasn't true.

Affirmations are affirmative statements or thoughts, generally stated with intensity and conviction, to help shift our mindset. They work by reprograming our minds to help us transform into what we want. But they can also backfire and keep us stuck.

I thought at first that if I used affirmations, I could change my business and all my problems would be solved. What I didn't realize was that my business was never going to make me feel better. What I had to do was to find a way to feel better in the moment, right away, no matter what happened at work.

I reached out to a friend, who suggested that I was starting with something that was too far away from where I actually was. While, sure, I might eventually feel it to be true, I wasn't likely to continue affirming things that felt like too big a stretch. It was like going from being totally sedentary to running a marathon without any training or warm-up. And so my goal became to stretch myself, a little each day, to affirm things that put me on the right path but that didn't make me want to quit after the first few days. My new affirmation—"I am doing the best I can in this moment for my family, my team, and myself"—was a kinder, gentler way of getting me to stick with marathon training, and I changed it up over time.

If the idea of speaking aloud something that feels lightyears away makes you feel worse instead of better, that's okay. Choose something that puts you on the path, but doesn't make you want to stay in bed. If you're feeling glum about your business, you could start with something like one of these:

*Each and every day, I do my best
in the work I have chosen.*
New opportunities are opening for me every day.
*New opportunities reveal themselves
when I open myself up to them.*

Then, as you begin to get more comfortable with affirmations and feel a bit better about where you are, you can level it up.

I like to write mine in a journal or composition pad, choosing each line for the affirmation. If there are twenty-five lines on a page, then I'm writing each chosen affirmation twenty-five times each day. I often like to work on two or three affirmations at a time this way.

You may choose to post yours on the bathroom mirror as a visual reminder to affirm yourself of what you want each time you brush your teeth. Since I'm very calendar-driven, I also put an affirmation I'm working on in my calendar so that each day, it will pop up as a reminder right around lunch time. However you choose to work with affirmations, I want to remind you to be gentle with yourself. When you're trying something new, it will feel awkward at times, maybe even strange, but hang in there. Our minds are pretty powerful. When we program them with affirming thoughts, a sort of magic starts to happen in our lives.

Affirmations are a way to trick the mind into what the heart already knows. As humans, we are pretty powerful, and we're able to program or reprogram our minds with simple statements. Yep, I said that. We can reprogram our minds. Just like a computer, we can transform our lives by changing the thoughts and words we use. Truth be told, the things that we say, both positive and negative, have an effect on our lives. By affirming what we want, in a way that states it in the present, we can attract it into our lives.

Early in my business, I didn't even realize that the things I was saying or thinking over and over again were actually affirmations. This was not what I'd been exposed to in my prior workplaces, nor had I learned about it in any of the books I was reading then. Little did I know that I was spending a lot of time, as many of us often do, reaffirming what I didn't like and complaining about the things that weren't working or the people I felt were causing me strife.

I used to say, "What have I done? Why isn't this working? I just can't catch a break. Why don't I have enough money?"–and then wonder why none of those things changed. I was conditioning my mind to accept that things didn't work, that I didn't have enough money, and that I'd made a mistake by becoming an entrepreneur. And I didn't even know I was doing it.

It's one thing to have a list of things we want to change, and to put that list out to the Universe for support and be open to solutions, which I highly recommend as discussed in the last chapter. It's another thing to keep ruminating over them, running that list in your head of the things you don't like, and beating yourself up for not knowing what to do to make them better.

Affirmations are far more mainstream than they were many years ago. Recently, my daughter Emily came home from school and told me her teacher had been talking about positive affirmations. It thrilled me that not only did the teacher share the concept but that my child recalled hearing about it at home. I always get a warm happy feeling when the kiddos repeat something I've taught them.

Why Affirmations Work

Louise Hay, author of many books, including my favorite, *You Can Heal Your Life,* is someone I consider the Queen of Affirmations. She explains how affirmations benefit our lives and how to use them to create the change we desire. She writes that an affirmation is really anything you think or say repeatedly, both positive and negative. She goes on to remind us that positive affirmations open a door and are the beginning point on the path of change. She gives suggestions for using targeted affirmations to heal particular areas of our lives. Her teachings of repairing or reclaiming self-worth are vital in creating a healthy, successful career or business.

I've used this in my businesses and found the results to be nothing shy of amazing. For years, I was attracting clients who were difficult, demanding, and appeared to have no interest as real estate agents in their buyer's or seller's happiness, just the fat commission check they would receive at closing. I found myself complaining about the way real estate agents were, how they were like those I'd attracted, and guess what? Yup, I got more of that.

So I met with my team, telling them I had what may seem like a kooky idea, but to please work with me and let's see what would happen. I asked them to describe their favorite clients—what they liked about them, what they admired most, the way it made them feel to work with them. We'd already had many conversations in the past about the challenging agents we didn't enjoy, so in this meeting, for the purposes of this exercise, we focused on what we wanted. I set the intention that we would attract more of those kinds of people, and eventually we'd be free of those who were not an ideal fit.

At first, several members of my team were concerned. Focusing on what we wanted would mean changing how we dealt with our clients, and it was likely those who were extraordinarily demanding weren't going to like it. One team member worried that her income would suffer if "Mr. Super Difficult" quit using our services. While she was frustrated by his aggressive need for attention and his endless phone calls that were all about him, she also relied on the income she received from his business.

Slowly we set some boundaries, such as giving herself permission not to answer every call he placed to her. Rather than entertain him while he was driving from one appointment to the other, she let his call go to voicemail. It turned out that the vast majority of the time, his message said something like, "Hey, I was calling to check in while I'm my way to another appointment, call me and let's chat."

She would sit on pins and needles, worried that he would be upset, but resisted returning his call right away. Same with his emails—she replied to them, kept up with the work she needed to, and delivered the wow service our company was known for. But she didn't reply within seconds of receiving his emails, and she kept things professional. Like many of us, she really wanted to be liked, by everyone, and found herself twisted into knots trying to make this happen.

I encouraged her to stick with me, and focus on what she really wanted. Soon a wonderful group of agents signed up, and because of the boundaries we'd recently begun to enforce, my team member had more time in her schedule and was able to take on this new group of agents, who turned out to be exactly the clients we wished to attract. The happy ending was when Mr. Super Difficult stopped using our services because he couldn't live with the boundaries we'd established.

One of Louise Hay's affirmations I've found helpful over the years is the following:

> *My joy allows me to express my talents and abilities, and I am grateful for this work.*

Another place where I've used and am still using affirmations is for positive inspiration in my home and office. Sometimes I find affirmations or prayers that are inspiring, other times I've created my own. I print them out, I add some pretty images, and make them lively and colorful. Then I post them around the house and my office so I and others can read them often. I even share them with friends, colleagues, and clients.

Your Turn

Now it's your turn. Think about the things you're saying each and every day, either in your head or out loud to others. Are they things you want more of? Or things that you'd like to change? Is there a place where you can reframe something you're saying to affirm more of what you'd like? For instance, "Technology is hard" (I hear this one a lot) can be reframed to, "I am receptive and eager to learn new ways to use technology." The former statement just keeps you stuck, but the reframe opens you up.

Maybe, if you'd like to make some changes in your business, you start with the clients you'd most like to work with. This isn't about marketing here, it's about how you want to feel working with certain people and affirming that they are there. You could also do this when you're looking to build your team.

In my role as a Business Alchemist, one of the exercises I often do with clients is have them describe who their ideal support person would be. In both of these scenarios, it's about feeling the way you want to feel when you're working with those people. To bring them into your work life, we begin to affirm what that looks like and how it feels.

Pick a few thoughts you'd like to change, and create affirmations around them. Use the way that works best for you to affirm them daily, either posting them on your mirror, writing them in a journal repetitively, or having them pop up on your calendar a few times a day. You could even create some artwork with your favorite affirmations. Use affirmations to help you create the shifts you'd like, simply by changing the way you think about things. If you feel your creativity is a little low, you may find picking up a deck of Louise Hay's affirmation cards a great way to start this practice in your life.

CHAPTER FIVE

The Big WHY

Ask for what you want and be prepared to get it.

~ MAYA ANGELOU

When I created my first business, I did it without creating a big picture. Heck, I didn't even know big picture visioning was something that I could or should do. I'd put together a business plan and had some ideas of what I wanted to do, but that was about it. My "why," my purpose, was as simple as escaping the place where I worked in the hopes I'd have more time to spend with my children if I went out and did my own thing.

To that extent, I did what I set out to do. I built a real estate transaction coordinating business even when several people, including my former boss, told me it wouldn't work. I provided a service that wasn't even part of the language spoken on the East Coast, where I worked—and I did it in one of the worst real estate markets in recent history. Best of all, once I reimagined my company as one built on remote employment, I helped a lot of women —including me—make an honest income working from home. We had more time with our children.

Was that enough? Things were going well for my business. I'd addressed a number of things that weren't working for me and made significant changes, and those changes were paying off. But my "why" still felt unaddressed. I was ready to take it on.

Writing It Out

In my work as a coach and Business Alchemist, I talk to many entrepreneurs who have a startup story similar to mine. It's easy to get so overwhelmed by building a business and putting out the fires that arise that you lose sight of *why* you struck out on your own in the first place. What was my purpose? I wondered. How did I want to feel as I navigated my days? I was eager to create a life I loved, both at my desk and away from it.

I began to make some notes about all this. I wrote down what I wanted to do in my work and in my life outside of my business. I asked myself how important certain things and experiences were to me. I thought about the people I wanted to spend time with. I didn't worry about how all this would come about, I simply focused on dreaming. I was interested to note that a lot of this had been in my head for a long time. I'd forgotten much of it in the business of being busy.

Unlike a business plan, which only defines what a business will look like and how to get there, this was the beginning of a plan for how I wanted to feel, how

I wanted to express my purpose in my life. I'd found success, but not true fulfillment.

Fortunately, the best part of being an entrepreneur is the ability to change the things we don't like in our lives and our businesses. Sometimes, it's also the scariest. Like you, I didn't realize I was signing up for a personal development and spiritual journey when I set out to be an entrepreneur. But here I was.

I call this process of identifying what we want, finding our Big Why and putting it into writing the Big Picture. Getting it on paper means I can go back to it when I'm feeling confused or frustrated in my business. It's what helps me make decisions and plans. It's what keeps me connected to why I do what I do.

The Big Picture

When we're clear on our purpose, on our Big Why, we feel fulfilled—and that's what the Big Picture is designed to help you discover. Without this vision, it's easy to just flounder around at the whim of what happens around us, distracted by shiny objects and being about as effective as a squirrel in the winter trying to remember where he buried all those acorns.

Your Big Picture is as unique as your fingerprint. It comes from your soul, and, when fully articulated, it can bring you clarity, direction, and fulfillment. Everyone has their own reasons for creating or starting a business. When rooted in our purpose, it becomes the fuel that helps drive us on even the crummiest of days or weeks. Knowing why we're doing what we do is how we stay grounded and make important decisions. Without this knowing, we have the vehicle (our business) to take us where we'd like to go, but not the fuel (our purpose) to get us there.

Over the years, as I've hosted workshops and met individually with clients, I've heard many wonderful reasons to start a business. Some of my personal favorites are listed below. See if any, or even all of them, resonate with you.

- **Give Back**—Maybe you want to help make the world a better place, perhaps through a healing service business, or coaching people through their own transformation, or creating beauty in the world through art.

- **Family**—Perhaps you're like one of my clients who wanted to create a legacy for her children. She wanted to teach them the importance of balancing family and or career, and knew she wanted to do it by example. Being able to check out for a few hours, go on school field trips, spend an afternoon at her family's favorite park or just being there when the kids come home from school is truly what she wanted to be remembered for.

- **Financial**—The amount of money you make is entirely up to you. When you trade your time for money, it's called a J.O.B., and while there's nothing wrong with that, it's not right for everyone—and that's fine too. When you have a business, your income is truly only limited by you. I'm not sure about you, but I've found this both powerful and scary at the same time. And since money is simply the currency used to get what you want and need, it has powers that allow you to help do the same for others.

- **Independence**—This seems to be one that most people I know want. It's a vessel that holds a lot of different dreams. Overseeing your future, your finances, and your time are just part of the independence you have as the owner of a business. If you're like me, you may chafe working for someone else. I chose to be the boss, and for the most part, I like who I work for. I'm sure you will too.

- **Travel**—Having the opportunities to do the things you want, when you want, means you can do the things that make you happy. Many, including myself, find that travel is one of the real perks of a modern business. Thanks to the internet, it's now easier than ever to run a business from almost anywhere in the world. Imagine, if you haven't already, working from a beach somewhere exotic, or a ski slope, or wherever your heart leads you. It's very possible, trust me.

In addition—and perhaps most importantly—working for yourself means you get to do something you love, something that makes your heart sing. Now that's what I'm talking about! Doing what you love is true magic, and I believe that's the most powerful way to change the world for the better of all humankind.

Whatever your reason—and it could be almost anything—I encourage you to stop for a moment, right now, and do the Big Picture exercise below. Define clearly why it's important to you. Please don't skip this part. It's the foundation for creating what you want in your life. After all, if you don't know what you want, how will you know when you get it?

One last note: After you've written your Big Picture out, don't just file it away in a drawer or leave it to be ignored in a folder on your computer. Consider making time every month to reread it as part of your planning. In addition to the written words, you might find images online or in a magazine to help you further define the feelings you want and create a collage. Take a picture of it and keep it handy on your smart phone. You'll find this especially helpful when things aren't going exactly the way you'd like on any given day, and you need a little pick-me-up to keep going.

As I mentioned earlier, when I began my entrepreneurial journey, I did a lot of pushing, forcing, fussing, and whining in an effort to create something, simply because these examples of masculine energy at work were what I saw in the business world. I often felt like I was swimming upstream in white water rapids with no life jacket, as if at any moment I would be sucked into the current and likely drown. The shift in defining what I wanted to feel and do has helped me craft a business experience that nourishes my soul and allows me to do work I enjoy while helping others.

Your Turn

Creating a Big Picture isn't something that you'll want to rush through. After all, planning a journey can be pretty fun and exciting, so enjoy the process. And please don't be like I used to be, and just read the book without doing this exercise. While you'll have intellectual understanding of the concepts, they won't help you nearly as much as they can if you do the work outlined in this exercise. I promise this is life changing. In all my private client work, this is where we start.

What you'll need:
- A journal or notebook.
- Colorful markers. I like the Sharpie fine point ones.
- A quiet spot where you won't be disturbed—ideally, with your phone silenced so you won't be distracted.

If the weather is amicable, I recommend you do this exercise outside if you can. There's something magical about being in nature that really helps us get grounded and focused. My favorite spot is on a blanket under a giant old tree. Where you actually do this is entirely up to you. Doing it is the most important part.

To start, simply take a deep breath, set the intention to become clear about your Big Picture, and ask for guidance from your Higher Source, God, the Divine or Inner Wise Woman (whoever you go to for guidance). Then, once you feel grounded, open yourself to the magic answers to the following questions.

A word here: don't judge the answers that come up. Just listen. Don't compare them to what others are doing, just check in with what feels right to you. If you currently have a business and the answers you get don't seem to align with what you're doing, that's okay. I was there once too.

- What inspires you or lights you up?
- Who inspires you and why? (These could be people living or not who you've met or simply read about. Who inspires you is unique to you. List them all and list why you feel inspired by them.)
- What do you do for fun outside of work? Or, what do you wish you had more time to do?
- Who do you most enjoy spending time with? Why?
- What is your soul calling you to do? In other words, what activity do you do that you lose track of time while doing it? *(Note: this may not be what you think. Please don't confuse your soul's calling by comparing it to what others are doing in their business.)*
- When you were seven or eight years old, that magical innocent age, what did you dream of doing when you grew up?
- If you had a magic wand and could change anything in the world, what would it be?
- Who do you want to be of service to and why?

(Be as specific as possible here. For instance, if you want to be a coach, and you feel you're called to do that, who do you see yourself working with? Women entrepreneurs, moms who want more in life, empty nesters, etc.)

- What scares you about running your own business? Or changing paths in your current business?

- What excites you about running your own business? Or changing paths in your current business?

- What do you want your life to look like, not just the business? (Describe the feelings you want to have, not the car you want to drive or the income you wish for.)

- Describe your ideal work and play day. (Don't hold back. You've got creative mojo here. Tap into it and let it out.)

- Why do you want your own business? (Even if you've had one for a while, describe why being an entrepreneur is important to you.)

Once you've answered these questions and maybe sat with those answers for a few days, take that information and write a paragraph or so to summarize this for yourself. Journal anything that you feel compelled to. While what comes up may not be clear today, trust me, it will in time. I've found that sometimes the momentum of thinking of questions like these takes me to places

I'd not dreamed of before. You are bound to have new experiences you will cherish. You will be more likely to do or try something new because you were willing to see things differently.

Completing this exercise is your first step in creating the business and the life you love, a life that is in alignment with your unique true calling. Take your time. Be honest with yourself. Have fun with it. Remember, there are no wrong answers! Trust the wisdom of your first initial response to these questions without over-thinking or comparing. The goal is for you to get clear about what you want and what is right for you—which, for the record, is generally *way* different than what is right for someone else.

CHAPTER SIX

Goals, Dreams, and Making Space for Magic

Anything's possible if you've got enough nerve.
—J.K. ROWLING

*E*ntrepreneurs are tempted to do it all, and I was no exception. Over time, I began to realize that I was engaged in so many business tasks that I didn't have time for the things only I could do, like writing, coaching, and speaking at events. That meant I was distracted from fulfilling my purpose, from being who I was meant to be and from doing the work only I was meant to do. I understood this intellectually—heck, my first business was helping others leverage their time by using our services—but it took a while for this to sink in for me in a bigger way. When I finally got it, I could feel in my entire body that it was a pivotal point in my personal and professional growth.

Let me back up a bit. When I started my business, I was genuinely resistant to the idea of scheduling or blocking off time, let alone making and planning how to meet goals. Sure, I had a schedule I followed and hours I assigned to specific tasks, same as my team, but I spent most of my time working *in* my business rather than *on* the activities that would transform it into what I felt it should be.

Back then, goals seemed akin to resolutions, and I'd given up making those a long time ago, as I wasn't good at keeping them. So I resisted establishing goals for myself, figuring I would disappoint myself by not meeting them. I dreamed a lot. I had visions of the things I wanted to do and create. I made enough to do lists to wallpaper my entire office, but I didn't put specific goals on paper, nor the steps to work to achieve them.

Maybe you're good at setting goals and love the feeling of accomplishing them. And maybe, like me, you're a wee bit resistant to the whole idea. People like me tend to be good at creating big visions, but are easily overwhelmed by all detail necessary to achieve them. It can feel better not to set any goals at all.

Dreams

Many years ago, a mentor of mine helped me see the value in setting achievable goals and then scheduling the action steps needed to accomplish them. Rather than simply putting something huge, like "write a book," on my goal sheet, she recommended focusing on why I wanted to write a book and how it would feel to complete it. Just as in the Big Picture exercise I mentioned in the last chapter, my goals needed to have feelings behind them to come alive for me.

When I focused on how I wanted to feel and why a goal was important to me, instead of on something external, I could then more easily take small milestone steps along the way toward it. When I sat down to write, I remembered and reconnected with the feeling. And something magical seemed to happen. When I got serious about the feelings behind the goals I set and started planning the activities needed to accomplish them, I found it much easier to stick with it. Because I wasn't trying to do it all at one time, I was able to break things down into smaller steps and step into that feeling in the moment. And by seeing the path before me instead of focusing on the finish line, I was able to find support along the way as needed.

For instance, when I was creating my first online course, Transaction Coordinator Essentials—a dream I'd had for a while—there were a lot of steps. I had to plan the course, create the slides, record the videos, find the best platform to manage the course on, configure the payment system to automatically enroll students who paid, and so on. Each one of those steps, and then some, were what it took to take my course from a dream to a reality.

Had I just put "create course" on the to-do list, it would have likely never come to life. So rather than that, I mapped out a plan that I could chunk down into bite-sized actions, some of which I was able to delegate to my team. I didn't know all the steps it would take when I started, but I wrote down what I knew. Then, as more came up, I added them to the plan.

All along the way, I kept reconnecting with why this

was important to me, and how it would feel to have my course available to the many people who'd been asking for it. There was a feeling of accomplishment with each milestone met, and I could look at the entire project and decide which tasks were to be done by me, because they involved teaching, writing, and recording videos, and what could be delegated to others.

By planning out the project and then deciding who would do what, I was not only able to create one course, I was able to create two, all while still doing all of the other things I did in my work on a regular basis. I blocked out time on my calendar, did a little each day or so, and before I knew it, it was launch time. As of the writing of this book, more than 350 students have completed the first course I created. And with each new student who enrolls, I am still celebrating and feeling how I wanted to all this time later.

Now I'm not talking about the kind of planning that means at 8 am on a Tuesday, two months from now, I will do a specific task. I know some people thrive on that, but I'm not one of them. What I am talking about is like a fun road trip: You've got your destination, and you've got your car packed and ready to go, along with some of your favorite snacks. You know where you're going and you know when you'd like to arrive. But by giving yourself plenty of extra time on that road trip, you can make a few stops along the way, do some exploring in a new town, enjoy some interesting food, and still arrive when you expected.

Along the way there may be a delay or detour, that's just part of the fun of an adventure. Now, that's my kind of planning. We'll get there at a predetermined time, and because we've left plenty of room for magical experiences along the way, we'll arrive with a smile on our face and a whole bag of stories to share.

Focus

Planning of any kind takes a high level of focus. Planning with room for adventure along the way takes a huge amount of faith.

You may think that maintaining a high level of focus is often easier said than done and that it takes practice. I agree with you. Focus also takes a lot of discipline. It takes discipline to demand privacy, to say "No, this isn't for me," to not react to the lesser important activities that try to demand your attention, such as new emails, ringing phones, and other interruptions. It takes practice to do this over and repeatedly. And it takes faith in your ability and that of those who are helping you with a project.

While we're talking about focus and email, please consider turning off the notifications on your computer and your phone. Do you really need to know every time someone sends you an email? I don't think so. It's often simply another way to be distracted and a habit-forming trigger that takes us away from what we really want to do. Remember Ivan Pavlov, who trained his dogs to associate mealtime with the ringing of the bell, eventually making them salivate just by hearing the bell? Our smartphones can have the same effect on us.

Here's a simple and effective way I've learned to help

increase your focus. Determine what time of day you're at your best. For me, it's morning. I can generally get more done before noon than at any other time of the day. Sometimes, I'll even get up very early, when my home is quiet, to write and plan.

Since I know that morning is my best time, I spend as much time as I can on focused goal-work, which requires me to be self-motivated and grounded, during that time. Much of this book was written in the early part of the day, generally shortly after I've meditated and had a cup of coffee. Then, in the afternoon, I like to schedule meetings, return calls, record my podcast, take a walk, and work on projects that involve others.

Speaking of meditation, I have a few words to say about it. Just do it! Find an app, take a class, make it a priority in your day, and watch how different things are in your work and life. One client I suggested this to reported back that it felt like a mini-vacation. Before meditating, she'd been checking her phone for messages and emails first thing in the morning. Now, she starts her day off with a ten- to fifteen-minute meditation.

You may be reading this and thinking, "That's nice, but I'm not a morning person." I know many who prefer to work nights, and I have one copywriter friend who is a real night owl, often working into the wee hours of the morning. She loves that she can work without the phone, family, or anything else interrupting her in the middle of the night!

Whichever time of day works best for you, morning, afternoon, or evening, plan your day so that your best energy is used to tackle the toughest activities. The tasks that require your concentration should be scheduled when you're at your best and when it will be quiet in your workspace. In other words, my friend, do the jobs that need the most focus and concentration when you're best able to handle them.

Focus also requires faith. It takes faith to believe that someone else can handle your less-important tasks and allow you the time necessary to focus on your soul's calling and goal-achieving activities. It takes faith in your dreams to limit or eliminate worry, which can often be the greatest enemy of this sort of concentration. It takes faith to sit down each day and do the work, even when you're not feeling like it.

As a goal for completing this book, I've gotten into the habit of writing for at least an hour each day, regardless of how I feel. Some days, I write and then the next day, delete it. I'm okay with that; my soul is called to write and so I show up on faith just about every day and do it. It takes faith to stop worrying about the future, which can prevent you from being fully present. The present is, after all, where you are right now. It's all we really have available to us.

We all have worries, and some are even useful. But as our mothers used to tell us, "There is a time and place for everything." We can't let worry distract us or rob us of following our true calling, of our goals, dreams, and desires. Stay focused on changing what you can change. Through faith and the magic of the Universe, miracles happen. Our job is to let go of the things we can't change. It's the only true way to overcome this source of worry.

Making Space for Magic

It takes commitment to take necessary action to step into your greatness. Desire is one thing, but unlike "the secret" in the movie and book of that same name, it takes more than desire to accomplish a goal. It takes a level of commitment to take inspired action, day in and day out.

With momentum carrying you in the right direction, you're well on your way to achieving your dreams and accomplishing your goals. Like I mentioned earlier, you're reading this book because I took inspired action to write it.

Breaking out of your routine, shaking things up, and stepping out of your comfort zone are some of the things that may be required to achieve your dreams. Trust me, waiting for someone to stop by, wave a wand, and deliver your dreams on a silver platter isn't going to happen.

To make space for the magic, you must also do things you haven't done before. You must be willing to be guided by your intuition or inner wise woman on what is the next right action to take and step out of your comfort zone.

Let me ask you a question: Have you ever gone somewhere that you haven't previously been, like a networking event or workshop, and found people who were excited to meet you? People whom you likely would not have met had you not attended that event? I surely have, and others I know have had similar experiences. Having faith, being committed to taking inspired action, and being open to opportunities leads you to these magical experiences that will help you realize your dreams.

While some take a dramatic approach to action by jumping in head-first, others prefer a "baby steps" approach. Either strategy is perfectly fine. Just determine what works best for you. If it's doing one thing new each week or each day, then do that. You may even want to enlist the aid of a coach or mastermind group to help keep you accountable and on track to reaching your goal. This method works best for me, and many of the clients I work with. Maybe you've found this to be your experience too.

Inspired action is generally a change from the way you've done things in the past. This is true for me. Rather than looking around at what others are doing and taking action to model that, check in with your inner wisdom and act based on that.

Boundaries

Here's a word of caution about change—and this is something I got stuck on for a while. Just because you're committed to the change that's necessary to reach your dreams, to taking the action you're inspired to do to follow your soul's calling, doesn't mean that everyone else around you is on board. And it's not your job to convince them either. The sooner I accepted that fact, the easier life became, and the bigger the opportunities presented to me in helping me achieve my goals.

Some of my friends and family didn't understand why I was no longer available for their interruptions at any random time throughout the day. After all, I was at home all day just sitting at my desk and I was the boss, so I could take time whenever I wanted, right? Or they didn't understand why I was going to another meeting or taking another business trip. Don't get me wrong. I'm not suggesting that you ignore your responsibilities or friendships, but being committed to following your soul's calling and changing your life may not sit well with everyone.

It's been said that it's lonely at the top. I don't think that's because there aren't enough successful people to associate with when you get there. Rather, I believe this saying comes from the people who choose to remain at the bottom, and always will, due to their lacking the belief, commitment, faith, and focus to change their lives so they can achieve their dreams. They want company with them at the bottom.

Inspired action comes from having a clear vision for your life, the work you want to do, and a connection to a higher source. It comes from believing in your dreams and surrounding yourself with as many people as possible who believe in you too. One powerful step I've taken is participating in a coaching and mastermind program. Having someone I can consult for solutions and sharing ideas and problems has been instrumental in helping me make substantial changes in my business and my life. It's also connected me to people who provide services I might be interested in, or that I can refer my friends and clients to. It's widened my network and given me community within a circle of women who are there to celebrate with me, and hold space for me when I need it.

Seek out a mastermind group (or start one), and attend events and training frequented by likeminded people who can help you realize your dreams. In my experience, the time spent in these groups can open doors we might not have even seen. Many years ago, I spoke up at my mastermind group and announced that I wanted to start public speaking. Within a few weeks, one of my fellow masterminders sent an email introducing me to a client of hers, which turned into an opportunity to speak at a conference in another state. *Reason # 811 to join a mastermind group.*

I had never spoken to more than about fifteen or twenty people at a time, and now I was being asked to go to a city more than 600 miles away and speak on big stage. Not only did that member of the group help open a door for me but also another member of the group was there to help coach me before the event. Saying yes to that trip transformed my life in ways I couldn't have ever dreamed of when I said I wanted to do more public speaking.

In following your dreams, your soul's calling, it's important to keep in mind that you're going to have to want to do the things that others aren't willing to do. This is where the support of others is critical. Surrounding yourself with likeminded people also places you in a position to celebrate and talk about your wins, as well as get input on how to be even more successful. While your friends and family may want you to succeed, they may also hold you back in an effort to keep you from getting hurt if things don't work out so well.

Get clear on your dreams. Write out your goals. Seek out successful people and spend time learning from them. This process doesn't have to be expensive, or even involve activities that you have to conduct in person. The process may simply play out in the form of a book, like this one, a CD, a movie, or even a podcast. Libraries are full of biographies and autobiographies of enterprising people, and those resources are available to us for free. Spend time with them vicariously through their stories, and watch how quickly things begin to evolve in your life. I once heard Zig Ziglar say, "In two years' time, you can receive the equivalent of a college degree in almost any subject, simply by listening to information about the subject in your car as you go about your normal travels."

When I quit my job, many people around me thought I was crazy. Perhaps, to them, I was. After all, I gave up what looked like security of a well-paying job to step into the unknown of entrepreneurship. They tried to be supportive, but still said things like "Hey, so-and-so is hiring. You should see what they have to offer. You may find you make more and work less." The other thing I often heard was how a big percentage of small businesses fail in the first five years. "Wow," someone would say to me. "Those are long odds."

Sometimes, after hearing such thoughts, I'd just want to scream. I knew that I wanted to be an entrepreneur and was ready to do what it took to make that happen. I hadn't jumped into this without deep thought and careful consideration. While I may not have known, and still don't, all the answers, I do know that what I am doing is what I feel my soul has been led to do.

Those people who thought they were helping me didn't want me to fail. But they also didn't believe I could succeed because of their own personal beliefs. It wasn't until I found other entrepreneurs like me who believed in their ability to dream really big and to go after their dreams with genuine passion that I felt better and accomplished more in my life.

Surrounding yourself with other likeminded, purpose-driven people also opens up a world of opportunities. Like I mentioned earlier, stepping out of your comfort zone and attending events can lead you to the right people for your business. Remember that it's not just the person you're meeting at the event or meeting, but also that person's network that you have the potential to plug into. Being connected to people who feature an address book of possible clients and resources for you is very helpful. It's also a place where you can be of service when someone says, "I'm having this problem …" Ideas and resources to solve problems are given and received without anybody being judged or made to feel like a failure. Like they say in the commercial: "Priceless."

Your Turn

Now it's your turn to make some magic. Get a big piece of paper that you can draw goals on. Maybe even a poster board size. Think of one "big goal" you have and write it in the middle of the page. Around it, list the several smaller goals.

For example, if one of your big goal is speaking on stage at a specific event, what steps would you need to take? You might get training, develop a presentation, practice in front of smaller groups, hire a coach, connect with someone involved with that specific event, create a speaker's page, etc.

Then, around each of the smaller goals, list two or three action steps that will take you closer to meeting them. Do this until you've gotten down to the smallest goals you can come up with. Then create lists for each day (or week) of things that you will do to complete those items needed to take you closer to your big goal.

Don't forget to include room for adventure, and support to help you accomplish this big goal.

CHAPTER SEVEN

Seeing My Business in a Different Way

Forever is composed of Nows.
—EMILY DICKINSON

o you remember *Alice in Wonderland*? One of my favorite spiritual lessons comes from Alice's encounter with the Cheshire Cat. There are a few lines in the book where we see the mystical brilliance of the Cheshire Cat, such as when Alice asks, "I was just wondering if you could help me find my way."

To which the Cheshire Cat replies, "Well, that depends on where you want to get to." Alice says, "It doesn't matter."

And the cat says, "Then it really doesn't matter which way you go."

It doesn't get any more brilliant than that. If you don't know where you want to go, if you aren't connected with the Divine, you won't get the intuitive signs and nudges you need to take you in the direction of your soul's calling. As the cat says, it won't really matter which way you go.

Knowing where you want to go and having a clear picture of it comes from creating your Big Picture as I suggested in Chapter 5. Here's your friendly reminder to go back a few pages, if you haven't done this already, and begin to work on your Big Picture.

Spirit

In the early years of my business, I kept my spiritual practices out of my work. After all I was striving to be a professional businesswoman and saw no one modeling any other idea. Sure, there were books about getting out there and making things happen, which I was deeply subscribed to, but most of those books made me feel worse about my life as opposed to better. Most of them had a certain "my way is the right way" arrogance, and some of the methods or ideas I tried simply felt wrong to me. Not wrong because doing something new was uncomfortable, but wrong because they were out of integrity for me.

One thing that didn't resonate was the idea of rigid scheduling and working excessive hours just for the sake of proving oneself. I'd started my business to escape that, to spend more time with my family, and while those ideas may have worked for others, they were totally out of integrity for what I wanted at that time in my life. And yet, sometimes I would beat myself up for not following the "experts'" advice, especially when I hadn't checked in with my inner wise woman.

Figuring I had nothing to lose, I began to use some of the spiritual lessons I'd been learning in my work. I began to see what I did as an extension of myself rather than something entirely separate. I began to show up fully, and with a clearer intention that the work I did was somehow going to make a difference in the world, even in just some small way, in one person's life.

One of the things I started doing was praying and asking for guidance—rather than simply listening to outside experts, I began to ask for wisdom from God on how to handle things that weren't working. How to help my clients and the team members I worked with best. While I continued to read and study with business experts, I stopped believing they were the be-all and end-all. I ran everything past my inner wise woman and prayed for clarity to take the right next step.

Through most spiritual teachings, we learn that we have within us a power that is greater than anything we can imagine. We call this God, Goddess, and a host of other names. As you can see, I mix it up. The most important thing to remember is to call on the power that helps you. This higher power can help you overcome every obstacle in your experience and give you feelings of safety, satisfaction, and peace, healed and prosperous in a new light and a new life.

This power can guide us, walk with us, comfort us, and illuminate the right path for us. This higher power can also help us in our work with the challenges that come our way as entrepreneurs each and every day. For example, one way I began to shift my concern about what others thought of what I was doing was to ask myself, "If the Divine, who is the master creator, is supremely powerful is for me, then who could truly have any power against me?" BAM! That, right there, is often enough fuel to get us through a tough situation. When I recall how loved I feel in connection with the Divine, I can't help but feel as if I have superpowers–and I suppose I do.

We have as much power as we believe in and that we embody as much as we allow ourselves to step into. I'm not talking about power over others. I'm talking about power within that will uplift us, that will inspire us, that will help us as we do the things our soul has called us to do. Our storehouse is filled with infinite good. All the things we wish for and dream of are awaiting to be awakened in thought to come forth into manifestation in our lives. The awakening must be within our thoughts, and our lives will then externalize the level of our thought. Limitations are set by us, and only us.

Mindfulness

As I thought about all of this and the impact it was having in my daily life, I began to have a more mindful approach to the work I did, the people I interacted with, and the clients I worked with.

One of the areas I shifted was how I worked with my team, taking a coaching approach rather than a managing approach. My experience with many managers in the past was that they were there to tell me what to do and when I did it wrong–not to foster a great work experience that would translate into a great client experience.

My team consisted of grown women who were good at what they did. They didn't need me to manage them in that way. What my team needed was for me to help them be the best version of themselves they could be in the work we do. Our regular meetings moved from discussions about clients to asking what was happening in their lives, what they were enjoying, and sometimes, what they were struggling with.

I hosted voluntary classes on goal setting, mindfulness, and even meditation. I encouraged them to take breaks, go for walks, and do laundry during the week while working rather than saving it up for their day off. I invited them to spend time with their kids after school and make time to go to lunch occasionally with friends. I celebrated their success. I helped them when they were struggling, and I listened deeply when they needed me.

I wasn't interested having a hierarchy in my company; I was interested in helping each person I worked with find the success they wanted in their work and their personal lives.

After shifting from working in an office to working from home again, I took an in-depth look at how I worked. It took a near breakdown, both emotional and physical, to show me that doing things just because someone else thought that was what success looked like wasn't going to work for me. After all, leaving a job that required 60+ hours a week of my time, only to do that again in my business, wasn't helping me live the life I wanted for myself and my family.

I'll never forget the night that Emily, who was about nine at the time, came into my home office one evening and asked me if she could have my credit card. I was surprised and asked her why. She told me, in the sweetest voice ever, that she was going to order pizza because it was late and she wanted to help me. This was a much-needed wake-up call and helped me see just how much of my old work life I'd brought into my business. I knew then how important it was for me to make my world a better place, starting right there in my home.

It was now up to me to use the work I did, the team I lead, and the clients we served to help make the world a better place. Not by being the company that had the highest sales or the most clients—I was beginning to see what I did as a way to change the way that business is done, how team members are treated, and even how work is handled. If I was going to stick with this, it would have to be different than how it started. It would now have to be based on more than sales. It would be about listening to the things that were important to my team and then crafting a way to do business around those.

Seeing things differently at work also meant I had to do things differently when challenges came up. One day, I was busy working on our website, trying to fix a formatting issue or something. I don't recall the specifics of what I was trying to do, but I do remember how frustrated I felt. I'd spent hours messing with the site, and it only seemed to be getting worse, rather than better.

About ready to scream, I got up and headed through the family room to the kitchen for a cup of coffee. On the way I caught sight of the DVD movie *Chocolat*, which had recently been given to me. It's the story of a woman and her daughter who open a shop in a rigid community that believes sweetness is a sin. As I came back though the family room on my way back to my desk, I picked up the movie and decided to watch it. Figuring I was already having a less-than-productive day fighting the woes of my website, I checked the clock to be sure I had time before the kids needed to be picked up. Then I turned off my computer and closed my office door.

I sat there on a weekday, in the middle of normal work hours, watching a movie. It was delightful. I loved the message of a woman following her heart and transforming the way her community felt about indulging in the sweetness of life. And I felt rested after the time I spent watching it.

Here's where the magic happened. To this day, I'm not sure how it happened, but I assure you that it did. After the movie was over, I was feeling a little better. I'd taken a much-needed break and was ready to go back into battle with the website. I turned on the computer, went to the place online where I'd been struggling, clicked a few things, and then hit Save.

It worked. The issue was resolved. It was almost like a part of my brain knew exactly what to tell my fingers to do, and, within a few moments, the battle was over. It was in that moment I learned a valuable lesson. When things get hard and you're not making progress, do something else for a while—like watching a movie that will help take you to a different place.

To this day, I've done this more times than I can count. Sometimes it's a walk around the block, a call to a friend, or reading a book. The idea here is that when we look away from the problem, when we do something different and stop fretting about it, this higher power I mentioned earlier can work its magic and send in solutions to those challenges. But if we sit there and keep fighting, we'll feel crummier and crummier. We'll doubt ourselves and we'll beat ourselves up. It will take us way longer to solve the problem—assuming we solve it at all.

Giving In Instead of Giving Up

It wasn't always this way for me. I used to sit there and fight the fight until I was completely spent or borderline hysterical. I was determined to make it work, rather than allow a solution to come to me. I fought so many unnecessary fights, and later, I'd make that fight ruin an entire day or week simply because I had an "it's my business, I've got to solve this" mentality.

I learned that one troubling incident doesn't have to ruin an entire day or week—it just took me a while to get there. I recall too many times in my life when I let someone or something that took place in the morning set the tone for the rest of my day. You know the things I mean. The laundry you ask your husband to put in the dryer before he went to bed, only to discover in the morning he'd forgot to turn it on, so the clothes you want are not ready. Or discovering you made a mistake in your accounting, and now your bank account is overdrawn, and you don't expect a payment for another three days. Even if you're not ready to forgive those you feel are making you feel the way you do, which I'll discuss later in the book, you can look to other places to feel better, to lift your spirit, and to bring a smile to your face.

Sidebar on emotions and sharing them: If you've ever called a spiritual friend with a challenge and they say something like, "Everything happens for a reason," or "You'll see the good in this one day," or my personal favorite, "You created this, you can change this," it's okay to want to smack them. No wonder we live in a society that hides our emotions—all too often we're made to feel like sharing our emotions means being reminded that it's all our fault, which I don't believe for one second.

When a friend calls with a challenge, our role is to listen. That's it. When we leap in with "helpful" suggestions, we're blocking the flow. It's perfectly okay to have negative emotions and to share them with a trusted friend, coach, or therapist. This doesn't mean you're not spiritual or you're creating something worse in your life. It simply means you're a human being.

Vision Boards

So how do you stay on track and keep your focus on where you want to go? One of my favorite ways is by making a vision board or a vision book, which is basically making your own book out of a photo album. This is powerful stuff!

While many think that vision boards are designed to help you attract things, what they truly are designed for is to help you attract *the feeling* you wish to feel when you attract a certain thing. I've met many women who've been fixated on the idea that they need to attract a tall, dark, handsome someone into their lives—so much so that they can only see people who fit that description.

Truth be told, it's not the looks they really want, it's a partner to love and be loved by, someone to share their lives with. They've misguidedly taken on the idea that a vision board will help them attract something very specific. Rather than letting the Universe bring them this—or something better—they are hell bent on getting the exact thing they've focused on.

I like to think that vision boards are a way to let the Universe know how you'd like to feel when you have or do something, and then for you to focus on that feeling by experiencing it. They are to help us see and feel things differently than we do now.

For instance, I wanted a four-door Jeep Wrangler for many years. I put it in a vision book, but I also described how I wanted to feel having this in my life. At the time, I lived at the beach, so the ability to safely drive in the sand was important. I also wanted something that said I wasn't like everyone else, with their silver, four-door SUVs, and that I liked having fun—especially with the top down. The feelings I wanted when I put this on the board were safety, fun, adventure, and uniqueness.

Once I articulated the feelings that would come with it, Beatrice, my Jeep Wrangler, came easily into my life—and at an interest rate of just over 1.5 percent, so the payments were easy as well. As of the writing of this book, I live in Chicagoland, where Beatrice serves me well in the snow and ice in addition to letting me have fun going topless in the warmer months.

There is magic in this stuff, and I can tell you from much experience that it works. Many years ago, I began cutting out images of places I'd like to visit, well before I'd stepped foot on an international flight or obtained a passport. I clipped images of China, exotic beaches in the South Pacific, London, Paris, and many more. I had them in a little box along with images of flowers, dream kitchens, and symbols that reminded me of peace, love, and harmony—things I really wanted to experience in my life.

Fast forward a few years and countless moves with this little box. I've added to it from time to time, especially when I'm teaching a class and the participants are making vision boards. I bring out my box and decide to create a new board along with them. As I pull out the images and start to arrange them on the board, I realize that I've traveled to many of the places I collected pictures of. I've experienced so many things I've wished for merely by putting them into this box, focusing on the feeling, and having faith. As I create my new vision boards, I add places that I still want to visit, things I'd like to experience, and images of feelings I want to experience often.

I like to update vision boards annually. My friend Rachel uses a book, and as she receives the things or experiences in that book, she makes a note next to them with the date she manifested them. One of my favorite examples is the table Rachel has on her patio. She'd snipped an image of an expensive teak table with six chairs so she could host dinner parties and spend time with her family and friends. One day, months later, Rachel was on the Home Depot website looking for something, and voila, she spotted an image of a patio table that looked almost exactly like the one she had in her book.

Best of all, it was on sale. It wasn't the exact table, but it created the exact feeling she wanted it to, and there was no doubt in her mind that because she'd figured out what she wanted, she was easily able to find it when the time was right.

I've had dinner around that table many times, and it's a place where conversation, community, great food, love, and lots of laughter are shared: exactly the feelings Rachel wanted to experience from the original image she'd snipped and put in her book.

Your Turn

Think about some things you can do when you have challenging situations in your business. I call this Emergency Funk Removal. On my list are things like call a friend, take a walk, watch a movie, or take a shower. By having a list handy and planning ahead for days when crap happens (because it will), you have ideas ready to tap into and a plan to help you get out of the funk. Let the Universe work some magic for you.

Bring in some spirituality and connection to whatever you believe in. Set aside some time to journal, connect, pray, or whatever feels right to you about what you're struggling with and the important decisions you need to make. Ask this higher power to guide you and give you courage, confidence, and whatever resources you need to do the next right thing.

Lastly, if you're a visual person or like pretty things, start collecting images of places you'd like to visit and things you'd like to experience. While Pinterest is a cool place to do this, you may find that having something physically front of you that you can see every day more helpful. You may even wish to consider buying an inexpensive frame. Sometimes, when I host a vision board workshop, I'll pick up poster-sized frames from Ikea so participants can proudly hang their visions in their favorite spot in their home or office as daily reminders. Remember, the idea isn't that you have to go to that particular city and stay at that specific lodge. If you want to experience what it's like to enjoy the mountains, ocean, or whatever it is, focus on what you want to feel when you're in that environment.

CHAPTER EIGHT

You Can't Help Everyone

You can't please everyone,
and you can't make everyone like you.

—KATIE COURIC

"Oh, the people she wanted to help!" For a while, I thought for sure this is what would be said at my funeral, followed by, "She wore herself out trying to help everyone else." It took me a while to realize that you can't help everyone. Not only are there some people who would rather you do it for them, there are others who simply love to complain and will do their best to prove your ideas won't work for them—even those who pay you for your expertise. In my studies and in my work as a coach, I've learned to not be attached to the outcome. But early in my entrepreneurial life, that was a foreign concept.

Perhaps I started off a wee bit naïve in business. Maybe that was even for the better, who knows. But I didn't realize until much later in my entrepreneurial journey that some people will take way more than they give.

I understood this intellectually, but I also naively believed that most people had good intentions, and that there would be an equal give and take, that the law of reciprocity would supersede.

Sadly, I was mistaken. As a recovering people pleaser, the people who took advantage of me were distractions to my desired goals and projects. While it initially felt good to be of service, it became clear that it was really more of a form of self-imposed servitude in an effort to bring in revenue. I thought I needed to be liked by everyone. And I believed that being liked would mean doing just about anything the client asked.

Looking back, I can see the error in my ways. I also know I'm not alone in this. Over the years, I've coached and mentored many women who go above and beyond just to keep a client happy. Deep in their hearts, they know this is not how it should be. In sharing this part of my journey, I want you to know that if you're like this, too, it's okay. You can change. You can shift the obligation you feel to your clients and transform your business into one that fuels you. In the following sections, I'll share some ways to do just that.

You Don't Need to Do All the Things

Early on, I met many people who wanted me to provide services other than those my company was created to provide. My business provided administrative support from contract to close for real estate agents. It was not set up to—and I didn't want to—craft their presentations, build their websites, or handle showing instructions. Yet I was often asked to do all these things and more by clients I wanted to keep and thought I needed to please, as well as people I met at events who I hoped would hire me.

This first came up was when someone I'll call Jeff complimented me on my website, which, looking back, was cringy, but at the time, given 2007 technology and my primitive skills, it was pretty okay. Scratch that, it was pretty awesome. I met Jeff at an event, where he told me about a new project he was working on that could mean a lot of business for my company. He just needed, he said, a little help with his presentation in order to cinch the deal and include my company's services in the proposal to his prospective client.

So far, so good, right? Jeff asked me a little more about how to position this to ensure that my company was included. He wanted to know how my company handled contract compliance, managed lenders, held buyers and sellers to agreed-upon deadlines, and made sure people arrived at closing with a smile on their faces. I happily gave him some ideas and shared a page on my website that detailed more of the specifics I thought would be helpful.

Jeff was old enough to be my father and had difficulty half the time just turning on his computer, so when he then asked me to help him put together his website in preparation for his meeting, I said yes. I figured it was the best way to make sure it got done—it was clear he couldn't do it by himself. After all, Jeff had promised me a lot of business as well as introductions to other prospective clients. In exchange, all he wanted was a few pages on a website, using the same site-building software I already knew. What could be the harm?

I soon found out. That site took me several long days and nights to complete. I wrote the copy, built the framework, scouted for images, and even re-wrote most of what I'd shared with Jeff from my own website to make "his" copy seem original—at his suggestion. I was genuinely flattered that he thought my site was good, and I thought he valued the services my company provided.

Jeff got a completely free website from me. And while that website, combined with his own negotiating talent, landed him the project, it wasn't one that was an ideal fit for my company. I'd done all that work for nothing.

On top of that, Jeff insisted he needed me to attend several meetings (at inconvenient times for me) because I was "part of the team," and he wanted to show the big shots that we were a united front. When things began to go sideways in the real estate market, my dealings with this guy put me in a place where I had to pay my team, even when my company didn't receive the fee we'd worked so hard for.

I didn't see it at the time, but looking back, it's obvious that Jeff wanted me for the project not just because I provided a great service, but because of all of the extras I gave away. Of course he wanted me on "his team"—I was working harder on his business than I was on my own!

This wasn't the first time this happened, and I wish I could say it was the last. But I had another former client, a man I'll call Clyde. To this day, Clyde remains a legend in my family as the client who drove me the craziest. I was always on the phone with him. Clyde would call from his car to check in on a transaction, maybe answer a question I'd sent him via email, and then, in the course of what should have been a quick check-in, I'd find myself called to be his sounding board on new ideas and even expected to conduct research on the fly.

I was flattered that Clyde valued my expertise. But discussing business strategy and marketing eventually led to me preparing flyers for events, promoting those events online, then emailing my list to help fill the rooms for him. I even showed up at those events to handle registration, only to go home empty-handed, since those in attendance weren't my ideal clients.

Fortunately, I woke up to the realization that I needed to focus my time and energy differently. When I explained this to my Clyde, he became irate. Funny how he was my BFF when I was jumping through hoops to do the things he wanted. Our call ended with Clyde saying, "Sometimes you have to do many things you don't want to do to make your clients happy, so you'll be able to feed your family."

Shocked, I replied, "I'd sooner eat cheap ramen than put my team through this." I honestly think Clyde was surprised by my finally standing up to him. It felt good to speak my truth and affirm boundaries. It wasn't too long after that call we parted ways.

Learning to Say No

By the time I started coaching and hosting mastermind events, I'd gotten a little wiser and learned to say no to the things that were not for me, especially when it came to the clients my team and I worked with. I'd begun to shift my idea of work and the business I ran from a hustle mentality to one of alignment. I wasn't chasing people or trying to get their approval. Instead, I was focusing on who I would like to collaborate with, who I was in alignment with, and how I could offer services that made sense to me and my business to help them reach their goals.

Even after all this, I still say yes from time to time to things I know aren't right for me. I've gotten better, and just writing this chapter reminds me of that. Not too long ago, I found myself on a call with Richard, someone from my past who told me about a new project he was putting together. He told me about the vast number of people he'd met since the last time we'd talked, people he would introduce me to who would surely want to do business with me. Almost immediately, I began to feel a slight tightening in my chest. Clearly, my body was trying to tell me something, and I was listening to it.

Richard made me a proposal. If I would help him with marketing and promoting his program on social media and to my email list, he would share my company's information with the people who came to his workshops. He'd steer them my way, he said, and it would help me get more business. To clarify what I was hearing, I restated his proposal back to him and asked him to confirm. Yes, Richard said, that's right. What did I think?

I'm proud to say I said no, that this wasn't a service my team and I provided nor one we were interested in adding. I knew in my heart that it wasn't a fit for me. I thanked Richard for his call, told him I appreciated him thinking of me, and wished him nothing but the best. For the previous six years, he'd been in front of many people who were my ideal clients, and he had not sent one referral my way. The only reason he was suggesting he do so now was because he wanted something from me, and he wasn't willing to pay for it.

When I hung up that call, I patted myself metaphorically on the back, did a very real fist pump in the air, and celebrated the long journey I'd taken to realize that I'm not here to help everyone. I can't do that—and that is totally okay.

Your Turn

Now it's your turn. Think of something you've said yes to, and then immediately or later regretted doing so. Sit with that for a moment. Where are you feeling that in your body? Think of another situation, and do the same thing. The idea here is to listen to the inner wisdom that your body shares with you. That same wisdom that is there with you at all times, trying to guide you and help you, even if sometimes you ignore it. When you know what that feeling is, and you're confident it's not just butterflies from excitement, but instead about something you genuinely don't want to do or that isn't right for you, you will recognize that this is how your body tells you. And then, all you have to do is say no to the "opportunities" that come along that you don't believe are a good fit for you.

Speaking of saying no, I once suggested a client repeat this word over and over until it became easy for her to say. It was also a great reminder that saying *no* didn't need to come with a lengthy explanation of *why*.

Saying no takes practice. When you're new to it, it's sometimes hard to do in the moment. When I was new to saying no, I started out by saying that I needed to check with my partner to buy myself some time. I didn't have a partner and still don't, but this was a way of giving me space to check in with my inner wise woman, my Big Why, and then make a clear decision, rather than impulsively saying yes to gain favor or make someone else happy. To this very day, when an opportunity comes my way, I pull out the Big Picture plan I have for how I want to feel in my business and my life, and then consider whether the opportunity will take me closer to that feeling, or further away.

CHAPTER NINE

God, Prosperity, and Business

*Success means we go to sleep at night
knowing that our talents and abilities were
used in a way that served others.*
–MARIANNE WILLIAMSON

I want to dispel a widely accepted belief that spiritual work is different from the work we do in our business. That following our soul's calling and offering our unique talents should be something we give away, rather than something for which we're entitled to be compensated. There's a mindset that either we have to do it all, be it all, and have it all in order to be successful—or that we have to accept a less-than-ideal lifestyle to prove ourselves to be spiritual.

I call BS. I don't believe that God, the creator of the Universe, or any higher source/being would want their creations to play small. This is a myth perpetuated for far too long in order to control people within the structure of organized religion. Truth be told, just about every spiritual doctrine talks about God being love. So why has religion turned this God of love into a God who finds satisfaction in our suffering?

In her book *The Divine Law of Compensation on Work, Money, and Miracles*, Marianne Williamson tells us to "…think of your work life, therefore, not as separate from your spiritual life but as central to your spiritual life. Whatever your business, it is your ministry." The first time I read this, I swear I heard angels singing—they sounded just like Oprah when one of her guests has what she calls an "aha moment".

Marianne teaches that work isn't separate from spirituality, but is interconnected. Whatever business or career you've chosen, it's your ministry. Whatever already exists is the platform for what could be—and being open to miracles is how miracles come into being. Miracles are what happen when you let the magic of the Universe do its thing.

Some people believe that they must abandon their current career and do something "spiritual" in order to feel spiritual—then they are disappointed when it doesn't work out. Williamson explains that no matter what work we've chosen, we can bring our spirituality to it. What if the Department of Motor Vehicles was staffed by someone you'd consider a light worker? Something tells me the task of going there would no longer be filled with anxiety and dread. Maybe our photos would actually look like the happy people we usually are instead of the mug shots we're most familiar with. And while we're on this path of imagination, think about the lives this light worker who helps renew auto registrations could impact.

We can't all do Reiki and teach meditation classes. We need light workers in many different places. Other work must go on to make our world work, and we need light workers there just as much as we need them offering healing services and trainings.

All You Need Is Love

I was in awe of the people of Bali when I visited the small inland town of Ubud several years ago. Each day, they created new small offerings as a part of their Hindu faith, a way for them to express gratitude and ask for peace for all. They didn't hide them away from the tourists. These offerings were an important part of their day, and they put them out where everyone could see them. I think this is why I loved my trip there so much. Yes, there was the tropical setting to enjoy, but there were also the Balinese people, who daily expressed their faith and lived it with authenticity.

Remember the Beatles song *All You Need is Love*? I know, who doesn't? Each time I hear that song, I see how brilliant they were. My favorite line is: "Nothing you can do, but you can learn how to be you in time," followed by the chorus. Love is the Divine in action. Putting love first is acting on faith that the Universe supports us in creating good. It's believing and honoring that we're here for a purpose, and that what we give we will receive, just as what we withhold will be withheld from us. Imagine the transformation in a world where businesses made love a priority.

Love doesn't mean we're giving everything away or that we don't charge for our services, as many spiritual business owners think. That leads to what I talked about in the last chapter: trying to help everyone and being fearful of saying no. In this chapter, let's focus on the principle of fair exchange that gives love to both giver and receiver.

Love allows us to wake up in the morning with a sense of purpose and energy. When we put love first, our creative ideas flow, and we're filled with powerful charisma, leading to new ideas, new projects, and new clients.

I've recently adopted a new way of starting my day. Before I get out of bed or do anything else, I send love energetically to the people on my team and anyone I will have a meeting with that day. That includes the people I know I will encounter on the road, the staff at the post office, the tellers at the bank, or anyone any place I will be going. I also ask God to bless all of them and look after them, and to guide me in being the best person/manager/coach/business owner I can to them. Then I lie there for a few more minutes and let it all soak in. I don't always know what my email inbox will have in store for me or what my day will be like when I get to my desk, but I do know that when I send love out ahead of my meetings and interactions with others, my day just goes better.

Love and Intuition

In her book *The Dynamic Laws of Prosperity*, Catherine Ponder, whose audio recordings I absolutely adore, explains in her lovely Southern accent that prosperity is everyone's divine heritage. "Success is divinely ordained and...poverty is not spiritual. Prosperity is not simply money, but also health"—and happiness, I might add. She explains that developing and using your intuition as a guide and understanding that prosperity comes from listening to inner hunches, a small voice, or signs from the outside world. When we ask for guidance, we're given it. But sometimes we don't listen or pay attention to the signs guiding us.

There have been many times in my life when my intuition has alerted me, but I didn't listen and only realized it after the fact. Once, I was taking Emily to the train station and we needed to stop for gas on the way. I generally use my credit card for gas purchases instead of my debit card, and prefer to go to one or two stations I frequent that I feel have a good vibe about them.

On this particular day, I didn't plan properly and ended up at an unfamiliar station. I didn't like the feeling I got there, but felt that I had no choice. I needed gas to get us to the train station. My first credit card was declined. So was the second. Oddly enough, both of them had more than enough credit available for a tank of gas.

I thought about driving off and going to another station, but I didn't believe I had enough time. So I pulled out my debit card and entered my pin number to successfully make the purchase. When I got back into the car I told Emily, "I didn't like doing that," explaining to her that people can clone your card and capture your pin number.

A few weeks later, I got an email followed by a phone

call from my bank. Sure enough, someone had done just that and charged more than $800 at a PetSmart in a city I haven't visited in more than ten years. Thankfully, my bank was on the ball and issued me new card as well a refund to my account for the fraudulent charges.

My intuition told me that using the debit card there was a bad idea. And so it was.

I've also received signals from my intuition in my business, some of which I listened to and was thankful for. One of these times, I was given the opportunity to partner with someone, but something didn't feel right and I declined—only to later discover that their business methods were highly shady.

On another occasion, I had the feeling that one of my employees wasn't happy with her job and wasn't getting her work done. I'd tried hard to motivate and inspire her, even giving her some extra paid time off to handle some family things, but didn't feel my efforts were helping. I was pretty new to being in business on my own. I thought I'd have to get proof by catching her not doing the work she'd been assigned in order to let her go.

I spent time looking for a program that would record the time she spent on the computer without her knowing it. That technology was hard to come by back in 2006 and very expensive to boot, so I passed. However, my intuition said, "Check her email." Since it was the company email on the company's computer, I did.

There it was, right there for me to read: an email to a friend telling them that she was looking forward to her husband getting a new job so he could support her and she could quit. Well, there is no sense in delaying the inevitable. I immediately contacted her, thanked her for her service, and told her she was no longer needed.

By doing this, I opened up a position to an excellent employee who became part of my team for more than thirteen years and a great friend on top of that. If I'd ignored my intuition, it's likely the excellent team member I have the privilege of working with now would have gone to work somewhere else.

There were also times I didn't listen to my intuition—and they ended up costing me time, money, and more. Now, I ask for guidance with each business decision I have to make. If the answer doesn't immediately spring forth, I wait until I get a clear idea of what my intuition is guiding me to do. Each time I've done this, I've been successful. Each time I ignored my intuition, I've ended up in an ugly mess.

Our intuition is intended to guide us in life and is there to help us connect with the abundance that is divinely ours. We must learn how to trust it. The best way I know to sharpen your intuition is to practice using it. I do this sometimes with Emily when we're driving. One of us will say, "Guess what the exact time is." We're both amazed at how often we're spot on or pretty darn close. We'll also do this when we hit the mall by guessing which row will have the best parking space.

When the kids were young, I used to load them into the minivan and hit the road with no agenda or destination in mind. We followed our instincts on which way to turn with having a fun time in a location we'd yet to discover as our only goal. As we'd approach an intersection, I'd ask one of them to pick the direction. We'd continue this until we found something interesting and decided to stop and explore. Sometimes I'd ask, "Which way is calling you?" so they'd think of it as more than just a guess.

Spreading the Love

One of my friends calls me the "Note Queen." My daughter Emily even counsels me to walk away from the stationary aisle in Target. She knows I can get lost there.

I bought my first set of notecards at a shop near my home long before I started a business. It was a fancy store that smelled like dried lavender and new paper, and I wanted everything in it. My budget said, "Girl, you are out of your league. Don't touch anything."

I didn't listen. I bought a fifteen-dollar box of floral, foil-embossed cards with little stickers to seal the envelopes, and I picked up the prettiest stamps I could find at the post office. I sent the first card to a friend who was under the weather. I mailed another to a friend celebrating a recent job promotion. I left a card on the desk of a colleague who needed a little pick-me-up, and another on the desk of someone who'd had a particularly bad day with a client. In each case, the recipient was not only getting something handwritten and personalized, which pleasantly surprised them, but they were also getting a little piece of my energy.

Once I opened my business, I saw the value in this kind of snail mail. I sent a card to each person I spoke with about my services, thanking them and mentioning something they'd said. If I had a coffee date with someone I'd met at a networking event, I followed up with a note card. I send out birthday cards to clients, team members, friends, and mentors.

How you may ask, did I send all these cards without asking for addresses? It's easier than you think. It takes just a few minutes to find someone's address online. Just look on their website or their business Facebook page, or do an internet search for their name in county records.

It's easy to send a text. It's easy to jump on the Happy Birthday bandwagon on Facebook. Both those things are fine, but there's something different about receiving something personal in the mail. I send out about twenty to thirty cards each month.

Once I sent a note to my friend Grace after I'd thought of her and jotted down something I wanted to say. A few days later, she called and said, through tears, "You have no idea how perfectly timed your note was." It turned out she'd had a challenging few days, and my note had shifted her energy and made her feel loved and special. Grace told me it strengthened her faith in the magical way the Universe delivers just what you need when you need it most.

When my granddaughter, who I affectionately call the Grand Ginger Princess, came along, I began to mail notes to her along with little gifts. I found out from her parents that she loved the notecards more than she did the presents. So, I kept sending out note cards, and now, as I travel, I take supplies with me to easily mail her cards from the road telling her I miss our time and to be good for her mama. If I can find postcards over the course of my travels, I send one of those too.

A word of caution here: when you send out notecards in business, write with the intent of letting your recipient know you're thinking of them and want to build a relationship, but don't talk business and try to close a sale—yuck! That isn't marketing, that's begging. Even if that's not your intention, if that's what your recipient feels, your efforts can backfire. Instead, mention something memorable that you discussed and leave it at that.

When my soul sister Sandy announced the opening of her healing studio on Facebook, I, along with many others, chimed in and wished her well. Then, as the Note Queen, I grabbed a congratulations card, jotted a note celebrating her, and put some confetti in the envelope. I held her card in my hands for a while and mentally infused it with love. I wanted to tell her that I genuinely believe in her and her incredible gifts. If I lived closer, I would have popped by with flowers. A card full of confetti and my energy was the next best thing.

Each and every day, your ideal client has hundreds of marketing and advertising messages coming at them—often from companies with deeper pockets than yours. If you want to stand out, do it by letting someone know you care. I believe our entire world could benefit from more love.

Sharpening Your Skills

Believing that a Higher Source is guiding me through my intuition, hunches, and feelings helps me make my way through life. When I trust my intuition, and things go well, I make a mental note of it and thank the Universe for the nudge. When I don't trust my intuition, I do the same. I thank the Universe for the nudge and resolve to do better at listening.

Trusting your intuition is just one way of attracting abundance and prosperity into your life. Visualization is another. Everything we invite into our lives is created first in our minds. We discussed affirmations, vision boards, and vision books. Similarly, focusing your mind's eye on what you want will manifest it more easily and quickly than time spent worrying or wishing fleetingly for a better outcome.

I'm not talking about making a list of things you want. I'm talking about visualizing how you'd like a meeting to go—not from a controlling standpoint, but based on how you want to feel. Imagine things proceeding positively, with the outcome you'd like to experience. Walk through the conversation in your mind and feel into the things you want to express. It's important to check in with your body as you do this to be aware of how you're feeling before you even step foot into the meeting.

You're here on Earth to thrive, not simply survive. While knowing what you want and focusing on it will likely attract it, if you do so without gratitude for what you have and without focusing on the feelings behind your desires, you risk ending up with things and experiences that don't make you happy.

Several weeks ago, a friend of mine, Robin, told me she was teaching her son about the benefits of compound interest. Robin was encouraging him to save his money while he was young and invest it in something safe, so he'd have a nice nest egg when he retired.

While I agree, I also told her that this was just one way of looking at it. I asked Robin to think about Bill Gates or Steve Jobs, who each took what little they had and invested it all into businesses that became hugely successful and allowed them to not only change the world but also give generously to those in need. What if they had invested that money safely and not chosen to pursue their dreams?

I believe that both these men were divinely guided and chose to listen to their intuition. Obviously, that choice benefited many. Sure, saving the money might have reaped the rewards of compound interest—but do you really think for one minute that was the "right" thing for them to do?

With hindsight, we can easily see that they chose the right path for themselves and that their work forever changed our world. But at the time, I'm sure there were many who thought they were crazy or even reckless.

It's up to us to trust our inner guidance, our intuition, and the Divine to guide us to the path that is right for us. I believe that this wisdom and guidance is desperately needed in business, now more than ever. I also believe that God wants nothing more for us than our happiness, success, and abundance.

We can be like stubborn teenagers, trying to prove ourselves to the world rather than trusting that there is a better way. When we need help and aren't sure what to do or which way to go, all we have to do is ask, listen, and be grateful.

What my friend's son chooses to do with his money is up to him. What's important here is to realize that there is no one-size-fits-all path. Each and every decision we make is unique to us. When we seek guidance from a higher power, and know that what we're doing is our soul's calling, the answers that are right for us come into focus.

Attitude of Gratitude

Gratitude, which comes from the Latin word *gratus*, means "pleasing or thankful." It's important that we express our gratitude for all that we have and all that comes to us each and every day. I like to think gratitude opens us up to more and more, better and better. When we are grateful for even the smallest of things, like a cup of warm coffee, a friendly smile from a stranger, or a good book, life just feels so much richer.

Several years ago, I started a simple daily practice of jotting down at least one new thing I am grateful for and why. It's shown me how prosperous and abundant I really am. When I have one of *those* days—you know the ones, where it feels like more is going wrong than right and you wonder if you'd be better off going back to bed or calling it quits—I still force myself to find one new thing.

There have been days where the best thing I can think of in that moment is that I didn't have to brush my hair before going to my desk, or that I could wear yoga pants in my office. And then, to bring my mood into a better place, I go back and look at the other things I've written down on previous days. Within five or ten minutes, my whole energy shifts and I feel the abundance I already have.

Abundance isn't just about money. It's a state of being, and it all starts with an attitude of gratitude for what we already have.

Your Turn

If you don't already have a daily gratitude practice, start one now. Make the time daily to note one thing you are grateful for and why. Stating the why is connected to how it feels to have this thing for which you're grateful in your life. Remember, even on tough days, there is always at least one thing you can find to be grateful for. Nothing is too small.

Prosperity is your birthright, and abundance is all around you. Ask God for guidance and help with your business and expect to receive it. Your intuition is the GPS for your soul, and it's the secret to a thriving successful business in alignment with what your soul is calling you to do. Always express gratitude for the abundance you already have.

CHAPTER TEN

The Power of Forgiveness, AKA Cleaning Out the Closet

With each act of forgiveness, whether small or great, we move toward wholeness. Forgiveness is how we bring peace to ourselves and our world.

—ARCHBISHOP DESMOND TUTU

AND HIS DAUGHTER

REVEREND MPHO TUTU

eing in business is the biggest self-discovery course I know of. Things will go wrong. Mistakes will happen. People will disappoint you. Vendors will let you down. Technology glitches are inevitable. If you hold onto all that, rather than forgiving those involved, you're going to explode—and it won't be pretty.

You, too, will make mistakes. You'll take action in a way that will later turn out to be a wrong decision. As the bumper sticker says, "Shit happens." This, my friend, is simply part of the entrepreneur's journey.

You must forgive yourself for your mistakes just as you forgive others for theirs. Holding onto anger hurts only you. It's a toxin, and it slowly kills. While you probably can't avoid getting angry, you can't dwell there and expect to be successful and happy. Anger is a normal human emotion. Acknowledge it and surrender it to the Divine for transformation.

I remember being angry many years ago when someone nabbed the parking spot I was waiting for, with my blinker on. It happens. But this time, it made me so angry I spewed obscenities from the car—windows up, of course, so only my kiddos got to hear me. After finding another space, I stomped through the store hoping I'd run into this person so I could give them a piece of my mind. It wasn't until we got back to the car and I began muttering about it yet again that my son Travis said, "Mom, maybe he didn't see you. Maybe it was an honest mistake."

Damn, that kid is wise. I wanted to retort, "How could he miss me? I drive a stinking minivan!" Then I decided it didn't really matter. In the scheme of things, it was just a parking space. Instead I told Travis, who was a little more than nine or ten at the time, "You're right. Thanks for the perspective. It doesn't really matter. I need to let it go." And I did. It didn't matter. That person I was so angry at probably had no idea how it was affecting me, and, even if he did, my job was to let it go.

Letting go doesn't mean you should try to suppress anger or any other feeling. This only leads to more problems. Anger is just an emotion, and it's okay to feel it. You don't have to deny something upset us or that something bad happened. Simply don't allow it to take over your life and become your story. You have free will, and God's help if you so choose it, to act or react to your emotions however you want to.

Here's the deal, my love. You are working for yourself, and you can't afford to have anything gumming up the works or blocking you. Forgiving *frees* you. It takes all that stuck energy and sends it off shooting into your business, your family, your *life*. When you're blocked because you haven't forgiven someone, you're just holding yourself in a place of unhappiness.

An Expensive Forgiveness Lesson

In early 2017, I was ready to take the information I'd been teaching in my business and in my first book, *The Road from Contract to Close,* and put that into an economical and effective online course. Someone I'd known for a while professionally mentioned on Facebook that he was offering a course-development service that sounded like what I needed.

We had a few meetings, and then he submitted a proposal. I signed up to work with him. At first, things went well. I'd agreed to pay him $8,000, and I was pleased by his progress. But then he started missing deadlines and meetings, and I found myself asking my assistant to take up the slack. I was hurt by his actions—or non-actions—and resentful that I was by then out a large sum of money, with completion nowhere in sight.

I met with my coach to discuss the situation. I want people to succeed, and so I'm forgiving of delays when situations come up. But by this point, I was not only out the money and time, I was also out the energy that I'd spent being resentful of him about his work ethic on the project.

What I had to do was forgive him before letting him go. I knew that if I didn't, I would say or do something I didn't want to when I released him. So, I spent some time working on forgiving him—on forgiving myself for making the decision to hire him. Then I set him free.

Yes, it still bothers me that he didn't do what he promised. And no, I wouldn't recommend him to anyone based on my experience. But I'm no longer angry over it. I've moved on, and now, it's just an expensive lesson.

How to Forgive

Things can radically change when you let go of what's been blocking you. Forgiveness doesn't mean you accept what the person did, or even that you ever want to see them again. It means that you're not going to let it control your happiness any longer. You're not letting it rule your life.

One hot Fourth of July, I liberated myself from some painful events from my past. When I'd woken up that day, I'd had no intention of undertaking such a monumental transformation in my life. But all these years later, the Fourth of July still has a special significance for me.

The kids were excited to spend the day with their father and to see the fireworks later that evening. I decided to deep clean my bedroom. I had a strong feeling that there were things I needed to go through, things that were blocking my energy.

I began in the early afternoon by picking up the laundry, washing the curtains and the bedding, sorting through magazines and books, and giving the bathroom and dressing area a good deep scrubbing. I was feeling very proud of my work. The room felt lighter and brighter and was looking really good.

As I leaned down to pick up something from the floor near my bed, I rediscovered some boxes I'd stored under there several years previously. Something within me said it was time to remove them from that place. I hadn't given those boxes much thought in quite some time. As I pulled them out, I wasn't sure what I was going to do with the contents.

After stacking them in a chair, I just looked at them for a while. There were five of them in various degrees of fullness. Several were bursting. I decided to simply vacuum under the bed, repackaging everything to make the boxes neater, and then shove them back under the bed. After all, they weren't in my way, and I'd done so much work I was ready to simply enjoy the fruits of my labor.

But when I lifted the dust ruffle and saw the clean space under the bed, I had an overwhelming feeling that this is the way it was supposed to be. That the boxes weren't meant to go back.

Many of the boxes were full of photographs, mostly of people I didn't know. I'd inherited them from my aunt after she'd had a stroke over a decade ago. Clearly, it was time to sort them out and decide what to do with them.

Soon, I was deep into purging and sorting. I found some photos of family members I hadn't seen in a while—

those went into a pile to be saved. The images of people I didn't know went into box for my mother to review. This went on rather easily for about an hour until an overwhelming feeling of deep, dark, sadness came over me. It wasn't any particular image; it was all of them—where they'd come from. They were reminding me of a time I thought I'd put out of my mind and gotten over.

Many of the photographs I was planning on keeping were of me and my family from when I was around six. This was the time when one of my uncles—the husband of the aunt who'd had the stroke—began to sexually abuse me. I don't believe he ever looked at these pictures, but the fact that they were in that house and were of me at the time of the abuse brought up things I hadn't felt before.

I felt sad for the little girl who'd experienced such horrific events for so many years. I felt sad for the sick person who'd done those awful things to me as a child. I also began to feel angry at the people who hadn't come to my rescue, and frustrated at my own inability to speak up and tell someone what was happening.

I knew at that moment that this was the day I would declare freedom from these injustices of the past. Somehow, they had remained close to me without me being aware of it.

On that Fourth of July, I cried. I forgave the man who abused me, my family for not noticing, and myself for not speaking up. I spoke out loud, which was difficult for me, but made easier because I was home alone. One by one, I named each person and the feeling of injustice I felt. I vowed to let it go so that I could allow that space within me, occupied by such awful darkness, to be filled with something loving and bright.

I don't think anyone who knew me then would have guessed that I held this kind of secret from my past. I appeared to be happy, successful, and full of life. I'd even believed that too. When I'd thought about the years of sexual abuse, I'd looked on them as sad, but mostly, I'd felt I'd moved on. Perhaps I even had, to the extent of my ability at the time.

Little did I know that while I'd done what I thought was right by moving on, I'd failed to take the important step: forgiveness. Almost immediately after I finished going through the photographs, purging those I didn't want and forgiving everyone involved, peace washed over me. I'd never actually felt that before.

Over the next few days, I felt lighter and lighter each day, as if something huge within me had shifted. And it had. I'd finally made peace with my past and was really moving on. I was no longer ignoring it; I was releasing it.

I used to think that sure, I could forgive someone who wrecked my car—it's just a vehicle. Or forgive the person who broke a special piece of glass I'd collected. But for so many years, I hadn't believed that someone who'd done something so awful to a child deserved to be forgiven. Surely even the Bible didn't mean we are supposed to forgive that kind of monster.

How wrong I was for so long. The simple, yet powerful act of forgiveness wasn't for him, the monster who abused me all those years ago, or for those who didn't notice. It was for me. Me, me, me—not him, not his wife, not anyone else, it was entirely for *me*.

The feelings that washed over me that day have remained with me; they are good feelings. I removed not only boxes under my bed but a pile of gunk within me, and in doing so, made room for something so much better. I took the darkness I'd received at six years old, removed it, opened my heart to light and love, and vowed to do my best to forgive others as quickly as possible. I liked this new feeling, and I started looking for others in my life to forgive. That work continues to this day.

How does one begin to forgive, you may ask? I say, in whatever way works for you. There are countless books on this topic. The following are few suggestions. If this is something you want to work on more, by all means, seek help with it, either with a trusted counselor, life coach, or in books and workshops. Forgiveness is some powerful stuff. Doing the work in this area of your life will allow for a much richer, fuller experience.

Declare it—Simple as that. Declare that you will no longer let it control you. Declare that you accept that it happened, and that though it wasn't right, you are ready to forgive the person who did it, whatever it was. You don't have to tell the person—in my case, he'd been dead for more than twenty years. But saying it out loud is beneficial. Declare that you will no longer let the past control you or keep you connected to it.

You may find, as I did, that the power you thought that person had over you dissolves completely with your forgiveness. You'll feel a sense of freedom in general, and from whoever or whatever hurt you. This may come about almost instantly, as it did for me, or it may take time. Either way, it's important to remember that forgiveness isn't for them, it's for *you*. Forgiveness is truly one of the greatest gifts you can give yourself.

Act like it -There were others in my life that I wanted to forgive, and I'm sure that there will be more as the years go by. One of them was my ex-husband. We'd never really been a good fit, but because we had kids, we felt compelled to stay together—him more so than me, but that's another story. I started to forgive him, and even myself, for the things that weren't right between us. I started to act like it as well. I didn't go to him and say, "Hey, I forgive you for all those times you did such and such." But I began to act like I had—really, for my own benefit.

This wasn't easy. At the time, we still lived in the same house. However, we hadn't slept in the same room now for years and co-existed as angry roommates instead. Acting from a place of forgiveness meant I simply stopped looking for reminders of the things I didn't like. I stopped looking for reasons to continue to loathe him and fight with him. For years, our entire relationship had been so filled with tension that we couldn't communicate without being short with one another or a fight erupting.

At first, I'm sure he thought I was taking drugs when he spewed something unkind and I didn't retaliate. Or when he left his laundry lying around and I simply picked it up and put it in the laundry hamper without comment. Yet, over time, with a conscious effort to act as though

I'd forgiven him and myself for our troubled past, things became much calmer between us. By the time I moved out, I was a different person.

Speak up—This is the one that I struggled with for a long time. I'm a bit of an introvert. Okay, more than a bit. I love to write, to express myself that way, but to speak up and tell someone, as I thought I had to do to forgive them, was something I couldn't see myself doing. How could I tell someone who hurt me that I forgave them for the things they'd done, when all I really wanted was to hurt them for it? For me, writing was the way I was able to do it, to let go of the things that I'd held inside.

My former mother-in-law wrote a letter to me after a weekend camping together at the beach. She may have thought she was sharing concerns, but it came across harshly and as if she were questioning my parenting skills. I was appalled when I read the letter, and instantly wanted to fire off a response.

Instead, I kept it in a drawer in my office and plotted for ways to use it to get back at her. I could make copies and mail it to all of her relatives! After all, they were all church-going people. Shouldn't they see that she wasn't living up to their standards? I wanted my revenge to be quick and painful for her.

Then I thought I might save it and read the letter at her funeral, so that everyone mourning this person they thought was so wonderful could see how awful she'd really been. But she stayed alive. Instead, I just kept the letter. Every once in a while, I'd pick it up and read it, recall the weekend, then put it away in disgust at her pettiness.

I may have also shared that letter with my several of my friends, who, gratifyingly, all agreed with me.

About thirteen years later, I came across the letter and read it again. This time, I realized how stupid the pettiness of it really was. There were complaints of a young child touching something of hers, her belief of when we should wake up while camping, and our children not being quiet at the campsite when they woke up so she could sleep. None of it even made a difference all those years later, except the fact that the words had caused a great deal of pain for me.

I immediately decided the letter was no longer something I wanted to keep. I took out a piece of paper, quickly jotted a note to her, and told her that I forgave her for the things she'd said. I wrote that I'd realized that the things that mattered were the people in the letter, not the silly stuff they did or didn't do while on vacation with her. I wrote in that note that I'd kept her letter for far too long, and that it was time for me to let it go. I forgave her and while I didn't expect to see her ever again, I thought she should know.

I mailed the note I wrote and the letter she'd sent. Instantly, I felt better—lighter—and I knew I'd done the right thing. I didn't expect to hear from her. But months later, she wrote to tell me that yes, life was more important than things, and she was sorry for the way she'd treated me all those years.

Now before you say, okay, Pollyanna, that's nice, but my situation/my past/my—let me stop you there. This is about you, not me, and not them. Only you can decide when forgiving someone for the something they did is worth doing. Maybe today isn't the day. But maybe it is.

I've used this exercise to forgive myself for the many mistakes I've made in my business. I've lost money, spent money I shouldn't have, made horrible hiring decisions, kept people around longer than I knew I should have, not spoken up for myself, spent money on advertising that netted me zero in business, and so much more. I've chosen to do this work of forgiveness to remove the blocks that continuing to stew over those things create. Sometimes, forgiving ourselves is one of the hardest things we can do as entrepreneurs.

I hope that the seeds I've planted inspire you and give you hope to make a similar transformation in your life. I can say without a shadow of doubt that because of this forgiveness work, I have opened myself up to happier experiences, greater joy, and more abundance.

Remember, this isn't a one-time thing. Issues continue to come up, and you have to forgive again. It doesn't mean you've done anything wrong. It just means it's time for you to receive more of the gifts that only come from forgiveness.

Just like our closets (or the space under our beds), there's only so much room in our brains for things from the past. When we get rid what no longer serves us, we can access all the things we want in our lives with more ease.

Your Turn

Make a list of all the people you are angry or upset with. This is your forgiveness list. Then, one by one, as you are able, say aloud, "So and so, I forgive you." Say this over and over again until you don't feel any anger or resentment toward them. You may even find it helpful to send them love and wish them well. Again, this doesn't mean you accept what they did to hurt you. It just means you're willing to release their control over you. Then cross them off your list and move on to the next person.

Don't forget to put your own name on that list.

CHAPTER ELEVEN

The Magical Space You Work In

*Normal is not something to aspire to,
it's something to get away from.*

—JODIE FOSTER

hen I left my career as a big city paralegal—okay, perhaps you don't think of Orlando as a big city, but it was to me at the time—I took home a lot of the rigidity of the law firm. Without even realizing it, I tried to recreate a professional office space in my home. That meant edging out my personality and preferences—you know, all that stuff that makes us unique. Instead, I filled the space with items straight from the corporate world, at one point even outfitting my family room with little cubicles and a fancy phone system. It felt familiar, but far from comfortable.

Thankfully for my sanity and the happiness of my family, I eventually stopped trying to bring Corporate America into my home.

Several years ago, I stopped calling the place where I run my business "the office." Instead, I call it the Magic Studio. The office sounded like work and brought up memories of places where I didn't always enjoy myself. In my Magic Studio, I create, write, coach, read, study, consult, and, most of all, have fun. I still say I've got work to do when I tell the family I'm heading in there, but most days it doesn't really feel like work. I'm blessed to do a wide variety of things I truly love. I even have a small print in my office that says, "This is where the magic happens."

Not everyone has a separate room for work in their home. When I started out, I didn't either. I had a tiny space the size of Harry Potter's cubby under the stairs in the Dursley house—and I shared it with my then-husband. There was a bifold door that protruded into the space—and when it was closed, the room felt like an oven or a meat locker, depending on the season, as there was no connection to the main heating and cooling unit in the house. If we were both in the room at the same time, the only way to get out of our chairs was to back out into the doorway. Tight and very humble beginnings, to be sure.

But despite the challenging constraints, this little space was where I began my entrepreneurial journey. I couldn't have been happier. Eventually, I made the family room my workspace. At one point, I even shared it with two full-time employees on weekdays.

The Energy of Spaces

Over the years, I've spent my days in a wide variety of spaces. Some have been easier to function in than others.

As of the writing of this book, I have what I believe is the best space yet of my entrepreneurial life, complete with a door that allows me privacy when needed.

As much as I love this space, I also sometimes take my office with me, and write on the patio when the weather is amicable. Much of this book was written there with my Yogibo lap desk, my laptop, and a cup of coffee. I find that spending time in nature is grounding and inspiring, and helps get my creative juices flowing.

Over the years I've learned that the energy of the place where I work affects what I do and how I do it. When my space was more formal and corporate, I felt I had to be that way too. When I decided to make it cozy and comforting and filled it with happy mementos, I felt better in my space, and my work came more easily.

Decorate your studio or workspace with beautiful things that inspire you and give you comfort when you're doing what you love. And make it your own. Pinterest and Instagram have lots of pictures of stylish home offices, but if they don't feel right for you, they're probably not. Don't try to replicate someone else's space. You'll probably never feel your best in that.

My desk is centered in the room with my back against the wall. I call this command central. I can easily see out the window. I can also see the bookshelves and all the other treasures I've surrounded myself with. A friend of mine who is a Feng Shui expert told me that having my back against a solid wall would help me feel strong and supported. Who doesn't want that?

I didn't consult a workspace designer, but if you feel

you need one to help you transform your office into a creative paradise, it could be a wise investment for you. You may also find that a few of the suggestions I share here will help inspire you to create a workspace you can't wait to go to, one where magic and inspiration reign.

Light It Up—Working in a dark space is draining. Your productivity will be less than optimal, and your cup of creativity will run low. I'm sure you've heard of the rainy-day blues, and often felt them when it's overcast outside. I know I'm not my best on those days; I want to curl up on the sofa or in bed with my favorite book and a cup of something warm to drink. When that happens, that's exactly what I do.

Studies show that the right kind of light will improve your mood and your productivity. But I don't think you need a study to figure out which light is right for you. Just listen to your body. If you're finding you're not as creative or inspired as you wish, perhaps it's just too dark or you don't have the right kind of light. I've found that natural light works best for me, and on most days, I don't have any other light on in my studio. As the day goes on, the natural light also reminds me when it's getting late and it's time to wrap up my projects for the day. Since moving to Chicagoland, I've invested in a Verilux Happy Light to help simulate sunlight on the many dreary winter days we have here.

Don't forget about fun lighting. This is your space, and you can decorate it any flippin' way you want. This is just one of the many perks of being an entrepreneur. Add some twinkle lights, or a chandelier, or maybe a fun, colorful lamp. Whatever brightens your space will also brighten your mood and creativity.

Bring in Some Nature—If you have windows, open them up so you can feel the breeze on a nice day. Pull the curtains or blinds back so you can see Mother Nature's bountiful gifts. Add a plant or two. They add a nice pop of color, and you'll benefit from the oxygen they produce. If you don't have a green thumb, there are other ways to bring in the outdoors. I have a clear vase filled with seashells on a side table and a dish filled with some of my favorite crystals on my desk. On my bookshelf, there are two small roses made of dried palm leaves one of my kiddos gave me many years ago. When possible, go for natural baskets rather than plastic and wood over laminate.

My client Lindsay has a very large stone Buddha in her artist studio that helps her feel inspired, creative, and grounded. She'd wanted one for a while, but they were priced beyond her means at the time. But when a nearby shop was having a going-out-of-business sale, Lindsay stopped in and there was the Buddha of her dreams, well within her budget. Her studio is her favorite place in the house now. It's also where she's likely to visit with you and sip tea.

Nature is filled with creativity and color. Infuse your workspace with its beauty and let it inspire you.

Give It Personality—If you own your place or have an easygoing landlord, paint the room your favorite color or colors. My studio walls are painted a light neutral gray and the ceiling is painted Tiffany blue. In the center, I hung an inexpensive chandelier I picked up at Ikea years ago.

Put up things that inspire you or bring a smile to your face. I have a Tibetan-style prayer flag hanging above my bookshelf with quotes that are near and dear to my heart. The green one says, "I am courageous. I am whole. I stand in my power." I also have fairies, hearts, gifts from my kiddos and other whimsical items, as well as a few magic wands I've collected. Think of your workspace as an extension of you, the place where you will do your best work. Fill it with some of your unique personality. My goal in my workspace is to feel good when I step into it. It sure helps me feel better throughout my busy days.

When I was trying to work from home in a "real office" and went all corporate, I hated spending time in there. At first, I couldn't figure out why, but as I started working in other parts of my home, or at a coffee shop, or even in a hotel lobby, I realized that my workspace was uninviting, cold, and more corporate then I'd ever wanted to be. One weekend, with the help of a friend, I painted the walls a soft green, hung pretty curtains, and added framed floral prints to the walls. Those small changes made me want to spend more time there, once it was more of a reflection of who I am.

Keep It Organized—Clutter slows us down and causes distractions. There's a meme going around Facebook that says, "The sign of a genius is a messy desk." I'm not buying it. No need to be a perfectionist, but having a place for things and putting them there will help you stay in your genius zone much more easily than when you're hunting for that important paper you've misplaced amidst piles and piles of stuff on your desk.

Invest in some pretty baskets to keep note cards, labels, or other goodies in. Use an old dresser you've painted for office supplies. Label everything so you can easily find what you're looking for, and for gosh sakes, when you take something out to use it, put it back where you can easily find it next time. Arrange your bookshelves so that they're not only lovely to look at but intuitive. Maybe even group your books by category or author. If you're not a naturally organized person or this all sounds daunting, enlist the help of a good friend, or find an expert who can help you. There are people who love to organize. Tap into their expertise and make your workspace one you feel happy in instead of overwhelmed.

Invest in Comfy and Beautiful Furniture—If you're like most of us, you spend a lot of time in a chair at a desk. Don't skimp here. Your chair and table or desk are important, and the energy you feel working there will be reflected in your output. If your desk is wobbly and unattractive, you'll feel that when you're doing your work, as will those you are marketing it to. If your chair is uncomfortable, that will likewise be reflected.

Comfy and beautiful don't have to cost a lot. If you're on a budget, try visiting a thrift store, or look on Craigslist. Maybe you can paint the desk you already have to breathe some fresh life and energy into it. I recently watched a video where someone had taken glitter and epoxy and transformed the top of their desk—maybe I'll tackle this in the future.

My desk chair was on sale at Office Depot. It was a closeout model and half price. It's got a high back, a big seat, and arms, just the way I like it. If your work requires that you spend a lot of time at the computer, as mine does, consider investing in a desk that you can easily convert to a standing desk. I did this a few years ago and try to stand at mine a few times a day.

Shut the Door—If you have a door, don't be afraid to shut it. I've told my family that if the door is shut, I'm not to be disturbed unless the house is on fire or there is a medical emergency. They honor this, for the most part—especially as the kids have gotten older. I've learned that in even brief periods of time, I can get more done without distractions than I can when I'm interrupted. Occasionally, I hang a sign on my door that says, "Shhhh, quiet please—magic being created" when I'm working on a project that I need to focus on or recording audio.

If you're worried about what your family will think, have a chat with them. Let them know that it's not that you don't want to see them or spend time with them, it's that you're working on something and need to focus to get that done. Point out that when you're given the time you need to focus, you can complete your project more quickly and have more time for them, making it a win-win.

If you don't have a door you can close, consider a screen or room divider to help you claim the space as your own. Even a pair of headphones and audio of some soft nature sounds can take you from the chaos of a normal house to a faraway place where you can focus and get things done.

The space you work in can and should be as unique as you are. Don't be afraid to sprinkle a little glitter in there and create some magic.

Your Turn

Think about how you feel in the space where you work. Does it spark creativity, inspiration, and magic? Or does it feel like a place you go because you have to? If it doesn't inspire you to feel your best, then it's time to make some changes. You don't have to make a complete overhaul in one day, but you could start by clipping images or snapping photos of things you see that you'd like to have in your workspace. Invite a friend over to help you do some organizing and repurposing of the space. Paint (and glitter for that matter) are pretty inexpensive. Set your inner creative genius free on some inexpensive furniture finds you've picked up treasure hunting at local thrift shops. You'll find thousands of videos on YouTube that will show you how to do this if it's new to you. Lastly, buy a plant and enjoy some nature while you're working.

CHAPTER TWELVE

But I Hate
Sales and Marketing

If we don't change, we don't grow.
If we don't grow, we aren't really living.

—GAYLE SHEEHY

As this book makes clear, being in business has been a spiritual journey for me. The way I work, where I work, and how I work are all interconnected with my values and my spirituality. And so it's not surprising that my ideas around sales and marketing have evolved as well.

I truly believe the more work I've done on myself, the better my marketing is. When I come from an aligned place, I attract better leads and have stronger sales calls. I didn't discover some sales-y gimmick or secret sauce and can now sell anything to anyone. It's more that since I got clear on how I want to feel in life, how I want to show up in my work, and the kind of people I want to work with, I began to experience more of what I wanted in my business. I wasn't chasing people. I was attracting them simply by being the best version of my authentic self, even in my business conversations.

If I had a dollar for every time someone told me they hated sales and marketing, I'd be able to include a gift card in this book for you to have a few fancy coffee drinks on me. Promoting our businesses and closing sales are things all business owners must do to survive—but they are also the things that challenge our self-worth like nothing else. Putting ourselves forward when we're not comfortable with who we are can make us feel like an awkward teen phoning a boy she likes and then hanging up when he answers. Oh wait, you didn't do that?

If You Build It, They Might Come

In the beginning, I did just about everything wrong. I was young and naïve, and I thought that "if you build it, they will come." When they didn't, I figured I had to chase them down. Boy, was that wrong. It didn't work, and it was soul-sucking to boot.

Back then, after I turned in my notice to the law firm, I emailed some of my very favorite clients and let them know about my new business and the work I'd be doing. I got lots of responses congratulating me on my new endeavor, thanking me for my help during the time we'd worked together, and wishing me luck. I didn't get one referral or client. You know why? Because I didn't ask. I just assumed people would get it and wave their hands to sign up. Big mistake.

In my first month of business, I ordered 600 post-cards I planned to mail to local real estate agents to let them know I was open for business. I spent hours designing these post cards and crafting a message about how great my company was. But I didn't have a list. In fact, I never really thought about who I was going to mail. I just randomly picked 600 people from an association of thousands and thousands of people, and I sent my postcards off.

I felt as excited as a little girl on Christmas Eve, anticipating all the calls and clients I just knew I'd pick up. I thought I'd have to hire someone almost immediately, so instead of working more on marketing, I spent time worrying over who I'd hire first.

Guess how many calls or inquiries I received? Zip. Nada. Zero! I spent all that time, energy, and money and got no results. Looking back, I know the problem was my random mailing list and my message, which was all about me and my company and nothing about the agents. But back then, I didn't know what had gone wrong. If I'd taken that money and tossed it out the window somewhere, I would have at least had some entertainment from it. Instead I got an expensive lesson, one I didn't even know at the time that I needed.

Another time, I was asked to speak at a local office about my company's services. Finally! I thought. I would be in front of a large audience who'd want what I had to offer. I had no presentation experience, but I said yes anyway. Then, in the belief this was how it was done, I prepared a detailed presentation of all the things my company offered. I imagined they'd be lining up to do business with me after the meeting.

It turned out that instead of a meeting with formal presentations from the vendors in attendance, it was more like a pep rally. There were high fives, cheering, and vocal celebrations for those who'd met a certain sales goal or recruited a new member. As I sat in the back of the room watching the scene unfold, I began to sweat profusely.

It was my turn to present. I was following an insurance agent who'd just given out dozens of $20 gift cards to local restaurants, gas stations, and coffeehouses and created a feeding frenzy in which he'd effortlessly captured just about everyone's business card and admiration. How was I going to top that?

I started out by telling those folks who I was and what I did. Thankfully, the leader of the meeting jumped in and started asking me questions. I think I might have passed out right there otherwise, it was so awful. I feel bad for the people who had to watch me. But even though there wasn't a line of people clamoring to be my clients, I did make a few connections that did result in clients. So it wasn't all bad. Thankfully, I've gotten much better at presenting over time, thanks to loads of practice and studying with others.

Then there was the time I was invited to co-sponsored a happy hour gathering for a group of real estate agents along with two other much bigger companies with far deeper pockets. I wanted to fit in and be one of them, so I said yes.

Network events make me cringe. I like people, but I

don't like small talk. I'm not good at it, and it's really hard for the introvert in me to stand around and chit chat. I can do it if I have to, just as we all can do things we don't like to when we need to, but this wasn't one of my strengths, and I was already worried about the expense. This was a recipe for disaster.

The event was held in the meeting room of a swanky steak house, where light snacks were served and there were several waiters taking drink orders. Unsurprisingly, everyone ordered top-shelf liquor. In fact, they drank as much as they could in the time we allocated for the event. Eight hundred dollars later (and that was $800 for each vendor!), I had nothing to show for my efforts except for a credit card teetering on the edge of my credit limit. Some in attendance thanked me for a good party, but they didn't become clients or refer anyone.

I could go on and on, but I won't. The point here isn't the mistakes I made, even though there were plenty. The point is to help you avoid the same and create the kind of success you want in your business.

Learning Curve

Clearly, the way I was promoting my company wasn't working. I had to start from the beginning and learn sales and marketing from scratch. I bought books and took courses and dove in deep. Some of them offered ideas that felt good and that I hoped would work. My instinct told me that others weren't right for me—but I usually ignored my feelings and tried them anyway.

In the end, I realized, I needed to make friends with

the process. That meant sharing from my heart and reaching out to people who I could help solve a problem. I stopped generalizing and hoping every real estate agent in town would hire me. Instead, I shifted to a narrow focus on the people I most resonated with and wanted to work with. I reworked all my marketing and sales efforts to attract them.

I quit looking at marketing as trying to sell something and started looking at it as education. It felt better to spread a message I thought would help people, that could educate them on options and provide my company's solutions to some of their challenges. After all, I'd wanted to be a teacher as a child. Why not become one through my own business?

The next chance I had to present at a sales meeting, I went in there with a heart-centered mindset. I didn't go in there trying to "kill it," as some marketing gurus recommend. I went in knowing that I had something to share that could help those who wanted it. My role was to simply share it with them. My presentation wasn't about trying to make anyone buy anything that wasn't a fit. It was about educating the attendees on a service, showing them options, and being there to answer questions.

It worked. I got a few clients that day, and a few more from later presentations. I knew I was on the right path. I no longer felt the need to get every business card from every attendee. Instead, I had deep, meaningful conversations with those who were most interested. Over time, most of them became clients.

Sales then became as simple as walking those I spoke

to through the services we offered, learning about any concerns or fears they had, addressing the ones I felt my team could serve help with, and inviting them to sign up. If they didn't, I simply kept in touch in a way that provided value in my follow-up, rather than always asking them to buy, buy, buy. I wanted them to know that I was thinking of them and rooting for their success, and that I was there when they were ready. I worked on developing a relationship with them.

That follow-up process I created often yielded admiring comments from the people I was trying to bring on as clients. While some never became clients, for a wide variety of reasons, many gave me referrals to people who did.

Attract Your Ideal Client

I got really clear on who I most wanted to attract as clients by using a method I'd picked up in a spiritual book on attracting a perfect partner. I wrote a very detailed description of the person I most wanted to work with. I described their personality, where they lived and worked, whom they had as clients, their business goals, and more. This became what marketing experts call my avatar—but I just called it my dream client. I figured if I were going to ask the Universe for something, why just ask for clients when I could ask for the clients I most wanted to work with?

Some sales and marketing books talk about finding your target audience in a way that makes it feel almost manipulative, as if you're trying to trick people into working with you. Maybe that was just how I read it, but rather than manipulating those I thought were best for my company, I simply thought about who I would most like to spend time with while doing the work I do. Who I thought I could help most, and who would value what I did. Those were the clients I wanted to serve.

Once I had an idea of my dream client, I looked to see where I would most likely find this person. I got really clear in my message and started connecting with people where I thought I'd be most likely to find clients who matched that description. Guess what? It worked! Not only did I spend less money on marketing, but my clients were much more aligned with my values. They were also much easier to work with.

Sales and marketing are essential to the success of all businesses. And with all the distractions out there, it's harder and harder for businesses to be seen. When we're authentic in our message and our services and know who we'd most like to work with, we stand a better chance of success from our efforts than if we try to be something we aren't. Doing otherwise is an expensive waste of energy.

Remember that there's gold in the follow-up. Over the years, I've learned that even people who are interested, who have challenges your services can solve and who you really feel connected to, aren't always ready the first time you talk to them. Sometimes not even the second or third time. This doesn't mean that you've failed. It means you've got to initiate a follow-up plan to stay connected and let them know that you're a trusted resource.

Like any relationship, it takes a bit of nurturing. All of your follow-up with your clients and prospective clients should be just that: a way to grow the relationship, deepen the conversation, and let them know you care.

Your Turn

Think about whom you'd most like to work with, your dream client, and write out a description of them in detail. Don't worry, this doesn't mean you won't be available for someone who doesn't tick all the boxes. This is to help you figure out who they are and then where you'll be able to find them. It also helps you clarify your message so that you'll be more likely to be seen by them.

For example, if I talked about real estate agents making more sales in my advertising, I'd attract clients focused on that. But I truly love working with people who are seeking work-life balance; sales isn't their number one priority right now. If my marketing and conversations with leads only focused on sales, the folks I most want to work with would be turned off by my message.

Ask yourself the following questions to help you tune into the dream client you most want to serve:

- What are their personal values as they relate to the services you provide? Be descriptive. This is for you, not anyone else.
- Where do they hang out?
- What is important to them? What are they like?
- What is the problem or challenge they're facing? What have they tried to resolve this previously?

- What are they most scared of?
- How do they want to feel?

Once you've thoroughly described your dream client, consider giving that description a name, like "Sally." You could also make a vision board about who you want to work with and why. Think about the clients you work with now. What do they have in common with your dream client? Then, the next time, you're creating a blog, social media post, or any other marketing piece, write like you're having a conversation directly with her.

If you don't have a CRM (customer relationship management) software program, consider investing in one. But remember to use it. Keep notes on your calls, set reminders to follow up, and use it to help you nurture relationships with your clients and prospects.

CHAPTER THIRTEEN

Time Management

*Reduce your workload by 30 percent
and increase your fun load by 30 percent,
and you will increase your revenues by 100 percent.
And you will increase your productivity
by 10,000 percent. (If there could be
such a percentage.) More fun, less
struggle—more results on all fronts.*

—ABRAHAM

he above is one of my favorite quotes from Esther Hicks and the collective she channels who call themselves Abraham. When we're working in our core greatness, when we're having fun and enjoying life, we're able to actually get more done.

Many years ago, I took a trip to Thailand. My plan was to work a few hours each day, mainly handling the things that needed my attention in the moment, as opposed to projects. This plan was based on the expectation that the home where I was staying would have internet service so I could stay on top of things.

But when I arrived, I was told the internet was out at the house and that the service provider had been called and would be there in a few days. Days! I shrieked. How could this be? I had a business to run, a team who expected me to be available, and work plans already in place for this trip.

After settling into the house, I raced to the nearest internet café to check my emails. It had been quite some time since I'd been in my inbox, thanks to traveling over twenty hours by plane. Funny thing was, there was nothing urgent there. Over the course of the next few days, I discovered the same thing. As important as my work was, so was my time off. I'd spent many days preparing for this trip and many hours traveling. Now it was time to have fun and enjoy it.

A few days later, the internet was restored to the home where we were staying. I stuck to my schedule of checking my emails in the morning and later in the evening. I stayed unplugged for most of the three-week trip.

If the internet had been working when I arrived, I would have spent far more hours online than necessary. There was some magic happening that forced me to see that all was well, and I could just enjoy the time I had in that tropical paradise.

Time-Resistance

Time isn't something that we can manage. I mean, it keeps moving, like it or not, and it doesn't stop and give us space to catch up no matter what we do. So, as I talk here about time management, what I'm really referring to is how we manage ourselves in the time we have.

I have a lot of personal resistance here. I'm not some-one you have to tell to be somewhere an hour early to make sure I'm on time. I worry about being available to my team. I tend to binge on projects—like this book. Right now, I'm rewriting this chapter on a Sunday morning. The house is quiet, as my family loves to sleep in, and my team is off, so I don't have to worry about interruptions.

For the most part, this works for me. I also block out some time a few days a week for quiet work, as well as keep a limit on the times I'm available to my team and clients. Truthfully, this chapter is more about called *time balance* than *time management*.

It took me a while to get comfortable with the way I worked. I've made peace with making the most of the time I have without beating myself up. Some days are far more productive than others. Wednesdays, for example, are when my granddaughter, Grand Ginger Princess, visits for much of the day. This means I don't schedule client appointments or work on projects on Wednesdays. It's quick emails and team messaging for urgent matters only.

The upside to this is that I get to spend the day with a little one who I totally adore. We play, create art, talk with the fairies, occasionally have ice cream lunches at our favorite shop. We even sometimes nap together. I plan this into my schedule. Sometimes, after her visit, I pop into my studio and wrap up some things that need my attention.

I believe time management is about choosing the most important thing on your list that day, and then, in the time available, giving that your all. Stay present. Don't think too far ahead to what's next, or let distractions get in the way.

Have you ever planned a vacation and, as departure day neared, noticed that you were extremely focused? You wanted to get a lot done so that you could relax and enjoy your time off. And, if you're like most people, you probably got more accomplished in those few days than you did during the weeks prior.

I've found myself thinking, "If I could just get that focused all the time, I'd only have to work three days a week."

I actually think that's possible. I believe that we are more focused when we have a clear vision about what we most want to work on, along with some space in our day for time away from our work.

As I learn and apply the philosophies of working smarter, I find that I can get more out of myself by using many of the lessons I've learned from others who are doing just that. I can now make one hour as productive as three or more hours used to be, and I can get as much done in two days as I used to get done in a week.

Imagine the potential compounding effect of working smarter in your life. How many more people you could impact if you had more time to share your gifts with them? Imagine also how much more time you'd have for other equally important things in your life like family, friends, and relaxing.

Work Smarter, Not Harder

Here are some suggestions that can help you get more done in less time.

Run the day, or it will run you. Part of the key to time management is staying in charge. Being proactive, rather than reactive, means being in control of and not letting others control your time. A favorite quote of mine: "Some will be masters of their time, and some will be servants." The choice is ours. But if we want to reach our dreams and follow our soul's calling, we must become masters of our time.

To master your time, it's important to have clear, written action steps toward your daily goals and keep them in front of you throughout the day. I've learned that it helps me to create each day's list the night before. Then, when I go to sleep, my brain can rest assured that I've got a plan for the next day. I don't toss and turn, worrying about what I'm going do in the morning. As you make your list the night before, review your goals, and prioritize your actions to move toward accomplishing them.

Careful about putting busywork on your list. Ask yourself: Is this a major activity or a minor activity? Is this something that I really should be doing to take me closer to the goals I've set for myself, or something I could delegate, eliminate, or even wait to do?

In my work as a Business Alchemist, I find many of my clients spend too much time on activities that take them away from the magic that only they can create. They're left wondering why they aren't living the life they want, or they're on the edge of burnout. They're cleaning their office, filing, doing data entry, bookkeeping, website updates, etc. No wonder they can't seem to make any progress on the projects they feel called to do! They're too "busy" to do what they want and too tired to do any more.

Often, by the time I meet them, they're about ready to give up. I prompt them to ask themselves the questions I propose you ask yourself every day and about every one of your activities. When you get clear, you'll stop substituting "busy-ness" for productivity, and you'll instead start to focus on eliminating the tasks that clog your day and keep you from reaching your goals.

Before you act, ask yourself: is this activity leading me to meet my goals, or is it distracting me from reaching them? Don't judge what you're doing as right or wrong. Simply notice what you're spending your time on and where it's leading you. If you find that what you're doing is taking you further away from meeting your goals, stop and take some time to evaluate why, or seek a mentor to help you discover what's going on.

Plan your day and take control of your time. Don't let the minor activities distract you from the major activities. Ultimately, you hold the keys to your success and accomplishing your dreams, not anyone else.

Don't mistake activity for productivity. You probably know at least a few people who always seem to be busy being busy. They go and go and go, and yet often have little success to show for it. They're like a dog chasing its tail.

To reach our goals in business and still have time

for living life, we must focus on the activities that yield the highest return for our time and the events that are in alignment with our soul's calling.

In my business, I've had the opportunity to meet with many business professionals from all over the country. Many of them tell me that their number one challenge is time, or, specifically, a lack of it. Together, we look closely at the activities they are pursuing, and start to find ways to improve their productivity. We look for things they can delegate, eliminate, or streamline. Often, with a few little changes and some virtual resources, they're able to dramatically improve their income and personal free time by working smarter, not harder.

Soul Sacrifices Are Not Necessary

Many people are so bogged down by administrative activities that they aren't able to shine in as the entrepreneurs they aspire to be. They're lost in the daily grind and not living their souls' calling, thus robbing the world of the special gifts they have. Most of them believe that the only way to increase their income is to work more, even though they're already working more hours than they'd like.

Be careful not to mistake activity for productivity, or movement for achievement. Evaluate the hours in your days, and see if there's time being wasted that you can otherwise manage better. For example, I know that I work best with deadlines and accountability. Having a coach or partner has helped me complete many of the projects I've taken on.

Check in with yourself. Listen to your intuition and pay attention to how specific activities make you feel. This will guide you to the activities that are most beneficial. Remember, there's an opportunity cost in every single activity you undertake. The time that you spend doing one thing is time that you could spend doing something else.

I'm pretty sure you'll agree that Oprah's not updating her website. Marianne Williamson isn't loading her e-zine into her email management software and hitting Send. Even if you have no aspirations to be like either of them, you can still learn from their examples. Marianne is on stage teaching each week because it is essential to her and the work she feels she's called to do. Only she can deliver the message the way that she does.

The same holds true for you and your gifts. *Only you can do that special thing you do in the special way you do it.*

For those who identify as a control freak, know that control isn't about doing it all but about identifying what's essential in order to provide your services or products in the way you want to.

Without focus, we're tumbleweeds rolling aimlessly around in the desert. I like to use www.brain.fm, whose library of music and ambient sounds are designed to help your mind focus. When I've blocked out an hour on my calendar to focus on a task, I set the timer on the site, put on headphones, and dive in. It puts me in "the zone," that space when time is standing still and things flow almost effortlessly. I also like to keep a notebook handy when I am writing or working on a big project. Then, when ideas pop up that don't apply to the work at hand, I can jot them down in a safe place I can go back to later.

One of the biggest personal challenges I had to overcome when I began working for myself was my feeling the need to be at my desk during normal business hours and then some. As if my worth or value to my company was based on the time I spent sitting in the seat!

One of my favorite business books on the topic of entrepreneurship and time management is the *E-Myth Revisited,* by Michael Gerber, which I have reread countless times over the years. Gerber tells the story of someone who opens a pie shop because she's told she makes great pies and people tell her she should sell them. So, she opens her business, works and works, and soon begins to resent the very thing she thought would bring her freedom. She tries to do too many things, which leaves little, if any, time for working on her business.

Applying this concept to my business has dramatically changed the direction and the personal satisfaction I derive from the work I do. There's nothing I feel is beneath me, or that I'm overqualified to do. But there are people on my team who do some things way better than me, and it makes sense to let them do them. My role isn't better than theirs. It's just different.

I've found over the years that mostly, what my team needs from me are quick replies to instant messages, which I can answer whether I'm walking on the beach, having a pedicure, grocery shopping, or sitting at my desk. No one really cares where I am, as long as they get the help and support they need.

Your Turn

Think about your schedule, about time, and how you use it. Are there areas where changing your practices would help you make the most of the time you have? Do you leave your desk or workspace at the end of your day feeling satisfied and fulfilled? Or are you overwhelmed by the countless tasks that need your attention and the interruptions that rob you of the focus you need to be your best?

Take a close look at how you'd like to feel in your day, compared to how you are feeling with the way you're working now. If there are places to change things up, do so. Over time, you'll find a balance that works best for you and the life you wish to live simply by tuning into the way you feel each day and tweaking things so you feel more of how you want to.

CHAPTER FOURTEEN

Being Supported

Surround yourself with a trusted and
loyal team. It makes all the difference.

—ALISON PINCUS

I used to believe that as a female entrepreneur, I had something to prove. And that the only way to prove my worth was to do it all. I'm not sure this was a conscious thought, but it was how I felt, and so it was how I showed up in my work.

As I shared earlier in the book, this led me to a miserable place in my business and my life. Even after I hired staff, I still worked much longer hours than I wanted to. Thankfully, with the help of a dear friend and mentor, I finally wrapped my head around the idea that there were certain things that I was great at, and other things I was okay at that someone else was great at. In order for me to continue to grow my business and help the people I wanted to serve, I was going to have to actually rely on support.

You know the funniest part about this was that my first

business was providing support services to real estate agents. There I was, preaching the benefits of using our services and how we could help them, and I wasn't taking my own advice.

Virtual Assistance

Part of the work I do as a Business Alchemist is help clients them find and eliminate the obstacles that are preventing them from feeling awesome in their work. For instance, my client Diane, a real estate investor, loved research—so much so that she was struggling to keep up with all of her projects and still find time for dating, which was important to her.

After digging deeper, we discovered that Diane got so wrapped up in research that she would get lost in it. She felt bad that her projects weren't completed as quickly as they could have been, and she was missing out on having fun. There was no balance in her life, and she was frustrated.

I suggested Diane hire a virtual assistant (VA) to help with activities such as preliminary research and gathering information. After some initial resistance, she hired someone to support her with the research she needed. She then committed thirty minutes to drafting a detailed description of each research project along with a video to show her new VA the steps.

Thanks to her VA's help, Diane was able to finish the research project the next day—and it was completed precisely to her specifications. She was blown away by how easy it was. Even though she'd resisted getting support, once the VA was on board, she was hooked. A few months later, Diane reported back that she was feeling so much more freedom thanks to her VA that she'd found time to date someone she really liked, and that it was going great.

Now, if you think that I'm going to tell you that you can simply get online, find someone for a dollar or two an hour, send them all the tasks you don't want to do, and then sip a tropical drink at the beach without ever having to work again, you're wrong, very wrong. Even a Business Alchemist like me knows this is just a myth. Even if you could find someone to work for peanuts, it will likely feel uncomfortable and wrong.

But here's my promise to you: Your life will immediately change once you finally commit to allowing yourself to be supported.

Everything starts with your belief system. Once you believe that it's possible for someone to help you—and perhaps even do something better than you—the way you run your business will totally transform. Few of us start a business so we can exhaust ourselves doing it all. We start because we're good at something and want to share that with the world.

Thanks to the internet, there are countless people here and around the world who can help you perform any number of tasks, both personal and professional.

Where to Find Help

I've worked with talented VAs in India, the Philippines, and Mexico, as well as with many based here in the United

States. My current assistant has been on my team since 2011 and lives in the Philippines. It thrills me to know that I'm helping her, and she's helping me. Like me, she is a mother who wants to do the work she enjoys and be there for her children.

Most of the VAs I've worked with are women. In fact, at the moment, my entire team consists of women. Nearly all of them have children, and many of those children are in grade school. The money I pay them enables these women to better support their children and families. The bottom line for me concerning this issue is that I'm pleased to be able to provide work for people who are talented, qualified, dedicated, and willing to work – no matter where those people are located.

I often meet people who tell me that they don't know how to work with a VA, or that their business is somehow "different," and they could never work with someone they'd never met in person. To which I say, phooey. If you want a successful, thriving business that allows you to follow your passion and doesn't mean doing it all, then you're going to need others to help you. It's just that sim-ple. The fastest, easiest, and often least expensive way to procure such help is to hire someone virtually. It just takes some creativity and faith to make it work.

As an entrepreneur, I love hearing the stories of other businesswomen. The other day, I was talking with the woman who performed my mammogram. She and her husband opened the radiology center about a year ago. She told me about the things she really enjoyed and that it felt good to have something of her own. She also said they weren't in a position to hire someone full-time, and she worked longer hours than she wanted to.

I asked if she'd considered hiring someone virtually on a part-time basis. Her first response was no. But, with her permission I spent a few minutes giving her some ideas. When I left, she was smiling and seemed to float as she walked me to the front desk. On the way, she introduced me to her husband, the radiologist, telling him I'd just helped her solve a problem.

Two good things happened that day. I got a clean bill of health, and I helped a fellow female entrepreneur find a way to be supported. Days like this remind me how much I love my life.

Let me emphasize this: If you're the only one doing everything in your business, then you are on a fast track for a breakdown. Having a business is about having freedom—the freedom to take time off, the freedom to make the money you want, and the freedom to follow your passion, the work your soul is calling you to do. If you're doing it all, that's not freedom, my friend. Having support doesn't make you weak. Support gives you the space needed to be your best at work and home.

When you have someone support you, you can do more things that fire your passion. I once had a number of short videos taken from several events at which I'd spoken that needed uploading to several websites, including our own. I knew what would happen if I tried doing it myself. I'd get busy, I'd get distracted, and it wouldn't get done. Or maybe I'd disappear down the internet rabbit hole and miss out on something fun.

I decided to have my VA do it. In the twenty-something hours it took her, I was able to write several blog posts, engage in three complimentary discovery sessions, coach a few awesome clients, go to dinner with friends, attend two business meetings, make several follow-up calls, connect with some friends and clients on Facebook, and get a pedicure. She got it all done, little by little, over the course of a few weeks. I got to do the things that only I could do. I was able to help several people with their businesses and enjoy some personal time.

It takes some planning, preparation, and commitment on your part to help ensure any new hire's success—and that's true when you go virtual too. It's time well spent. You can create your own SOP (standard operating procedure) that specifies how you want things done. Sometimes you can find a book or online course on a specific business topic (like SEO, marketing, or social media) that you can hire someone to review, determine the necessary action steps, and then help you implement. Knowledge alone isn't power, but knowledge with action is.

Being supported doesn't make you weak or diminish the fact that this is your business, one you built. Getting support allows you to make a bigger impact on the world with your special gifts and talents, while allowing you the time to do the things that help you be your best.

Your Turn

Think of the tasks you need help with, then reach out to your network for leads on a good virtual support assistant who can help. Start by assigning small tasks and work your way up to bigger and more complex ones as you get better at being supported and feel more comfortable with the process. Don't get discouraged if the first person you hire doesn't wow you. Go back and look over your directions, see if there was more you could have provided, and ask this person what they need to do better. If they aren't a match, try again. I promise you, you'll feel better in your work, you'll have more time for fun, and you'll be able to share more of your special gifts with the world when you find the right support.

If you need more inspiration and guidance on this, head over to my website, www.MichelleSpalding.com, and pick up the workbook and MP3 called *Soul Crafted Success* where I go deep into this topic.

CHAPTER FIFTEEN

When the Shit Hits the Fan

I'm glad I didn't know
The way it all would end, the way it all would go
Our lives are better left to chance
I could have missed the pain
But I'd have to miss the dance.

–GARTH BROOKS, *THE DANCE*

*H*onestly, I think if I'd known all the things that would happen, I might not have taken this crazy journey of an entrepreneur. But then again, I think that Garth Brooks says it best about the experiences of the unknown and being grateful for them. The song quoted above is about a failed romance. He's glad he didn't know how it was going to come out because he'd have missed the dance. I feel this way about my fourteen-plus years of entrepreneurship.

Crash!

When I started out way back in 2005, I had no idea that a few short years later, just as things were coming together in my business, the worst real estate crash since the Great Depression would hit. Instead of experiencing the closings my team had worked hard on funding and buyers getting the keys to their new condo, we got faxes from lenders saying they'd gone out of business. I joke, "If my crystal ball had only been working when I decided to open my business..." And yet, if it had, I'd have missed this dance.

Since things were so tight for real estate agents, who were my primary clients, they weren't exactly lining up to pay for our services when they had more time than money. I'd be lying if I said I didn't cry a lot. I had children to feed, a team to pay, and more bills than I seemed to have money to cover. Since I had no plans of giving up or walking away, I had to get creative.

What ended up saving my business was looking outside the area, taking a trip to another city, and marketing there for new clients. The Florida real estate market was hit hard, but the Maryland and Washington DC markets were still doing well. Even in hard economic times, there were people moving in and out of our nation's capital.

I took a gamble. I went to an event, made some new connections, and picked up some new clients. I even got to spend a few days in DC touring the museums and monuments. That was one dance I didn't see happening when I opened the doors, but it taught me a lot about creativity, resourcefulness, and how to work outside of my local area. Rather than joining the doom and gloom band wagon, as many in my industry had, I sought a creative solution to a problem I had no control over.

People Problems

There were other times when I felt like being an entrepreneur wasn't for me. One time, as I pulled up to a speaking event about three hours from my home, my phone rang. My client Barbara wasn't happy with the level of service she'd been receiving from one of my team members, and the situation needed my immediate attention. Quickly I jumped into action to help, re-assigned Barbara to another team member, and then set out to give my talk.

On the way home, Barbara called me and thanked me for handling things so quickly. She was impressed. Grateful that Barbara had given us another chance, I again tried to reach out to Kim, the original team member she'd been assigned. I had no success in reaching Kim by email or by phone. Odd, I thought, and continued home hoping she was okay.

The next morning I reviewed Kim's files, emails, and call logs, only to discover she'd pretty much been checked out for the last few days without letting me know she needed coverage. I also discovered an email confirming flight information from an old beau Kim had apparently reconnected with, as well as her message to him that she would have plenty of time to play while he was in town and her kiddos were in school. Disturbed that Kim had let her professional obligations slide, I blocked her access to her email, our phone system, and the files. I didn't have her cell number, so I had no way to contact her to let her know.

A few days later, I got a Skype IM from Kim asking if her email password had been changed. Right there, on Skype, I had to let her know she was no longer a part of our team. I think she knew it was coming. After this, I adopted a better policy of collecting team member contact information. If only Kim had asked for time off, rather than dodging responsibilities. Barbara, the client in question, was important. She was new to us at the time, but would go on to work with us for another twelve years.

Another time, someone I loved dearly broke my heart, someone who'd been my best friend and lover for many years. We'd traveled the world together, moved to the beach (which was our favorite place) twice, and spent hours talking business—we were both entrepreneurs. One day, he decided it was time for him to move on. I was heartbroken, to say the least, and had no idea what to do with myself. I'm not good at reaching out to people in times of trouble. I can spend too much time in my head trying to solve problems rather than allowing others to support me. But that day, I knew I needed help.

I reached out to a few women and let myself cry on their shoulder. I didn't try to be anything. I just felt what I was feeling. Those women were there for me, and I was beyond grateful for them. I reached out to a few of my long-time team members and asked them for support with some work tasks. I canceled several meetings as well, letting people know an emergency had come up that needed my attention and that I would reschedule as soon as possible.

Willing to See Things Differently

A few days later, after crying until I didn't think I had anything left in my body to produce another tear, I took a long walk on the beach. As I walked, I recited a prayer that Marianne Williamson had shared in a video about relationships: "Dear God, I am willing to see things differently." I must have repeated that about 500 times—no exaggeration.

Soon after returning home, I felt peace wash over me and had an inner knowing that all would be well. In what can only be described as a *whoosh*, I knew I was on a path to healing my broken heart and no longer feared whatever was next. I can only explain that moment as a miracle, which, as we learn from *A Course in Miracles*, is simply a shift in perspective from fear to love.

I believe that much of that has to do with the space I made in my day and my willingness to feel my way through this tough time. While I was still quite sad, I was also comforted by the miraculous experience I'd just had. I still had no idea how or when I would get through this— or even what it would look like. But I had a knowing that all would be well, and that comforted me. I think if I had pushed ahead in work, kept going and didn't take time off, I wouldn't have had the space I needed for that miracle on the beach.

There've been other crises I thought would derail me, like when my website was under attack—literally. There were bots targeting it and doing their best to access it, for reasons unknown to me—I mean, who's really that interested in real estate transaction coordinating? But those attacks were causing my website to crash multiple times each day, and people who'd paid to access my courses weren't able to view them.

Each day, I tried something new to resolve the situation while praying that I wouldn't get another email or IM from a customer telling me they couldn't access their course. My team and I spoke with our hosting company, read blog after blog about possible solutions, hired two different experts to work on it, and, in the end, the situation was finally resolved. Another time when, if I'd known going into it would have been as hard as it was, I might not have danced.

Mess and Miracles

Shit happens. Life is messy and business is messy. No one escapes this. But miracles also happen, each and every day. It's up to us to allow them in. Even the most soulful of businesses have challenges. It doesn't mean we're not doing the things our soul has called us to do. Hard times are just a speed hump or detour along the way. To go back to Garth's metaphor, challenges are just an extended version of the song, and we've got some extra dancing to do.

When the shit hits the fan, it's messy, and it takes a lot of work to clean it up. Work it's almost impossible to carry out by ourselves. When challenges arise, even when they're personal, it's impossible for them not to affect our work. We can either let those we work with know we're not our best right now, and briefly explain why, or we can shut down, plow ahead, and pretend nothing is wrong.

I don't recommend the latter. It can alienate a trusted colleague, and it's inauthentic. While we may say we're fine, our bodies and our energy won't lie. People will know something is off. I'm not saying we need to air our dirty laundry to those we don't feel close to. But when we're not ourselves and going through something, we should be able to say that, and be given some grace in our work and for ourselves.

The same holds true for the people we work with. When things aren't well with them, we can hold the same space for them, extend grace, and let them know we are there for them. Imagine how much faster people could heal and work through situations if we didn't have to hide them or stew about them in silence.

With today's social media, we have the ability to connect and share in an instant. Some of us share authentically; some of us put on a good front. I'm not saying we need to share heartache and sadness with everyone we're friends with on Facebook. But it helps to understand that what we're seeing from others isn't the whole picture. When you compare yourself, your progress, and your path to others, you're setting yourself up for struggle.

Maybe your sales won't grow every year. Maybe each year isn't always better than the last. That doesn't mean you aren't successful. If you're doing what your soul has called you to do, if you're spending time with people you love, if you're healthy—how is that not success?

I can say without a doubt that some of the biggest

struggles I've experienced in life and business have been easier to get through with the help of a coach, mentor, or mastermind group. Being able to bring a situation to someone I trust, someone who knows me well and wants to see me succeed, has not only helped me resolve many a challenge but also helped me see that this too, shall pass. Maybe like a kidney stone, with some pain, but I can get through it.

My mentors, coaches, and fellow masterminders have been the same people with whom I celebrate the miracles that have shown up for me. In my role as a Business Alchemist, I, too, have the honor of seeing others through challenging situations and celebrating with them as they make progress in moving forward. It's my privilege to help them see the miracles and navigate the messes.

Celebrating the Mess and Miracles

What if we took a different approach to all of this? Maybe it's high time we started to celebrate the mess, not for the mess itself, but for the fact that we survived it, even when we thought all hope was lost. Perhaps it's time we held space for people who are in the midst of a mess and just let them know we care instead of trying to fix it or, worse yet, telling them that "everything happens for a reason." No one wants to hear that when they are in the midst of a shit storm.

And maybe it's time we realized that, well, shit happens. Be honest with people when it does. Ask for support from a coach or mentor. Accept support where it's offered and feels right for you. And, most of all, show yourself a huge amount of grace and compassion. After all, what good is life if we can't be our authentic selves in it?

Feel all the feels, good, bad, and ugly. That's how life is fully experienced. So dance the dance, enjoying each moment to the fullest, knowing that while it may not go as expected, you'll have the experience to cherish forever.

Your Turn

Think back the circumstances you've survived that, at the time, felt crippling. Think of the things you've accomplished, even when the cards were stacked against you. Think about the many people you've been there for, when they were having a difficult time—and those who have been there for you.

Make a list of all of it, a sort of a personal brag book, and begin to feel into the many examples in your life. Use this list as a reminder to yourself of just how amazing you are. Reach for it when you're having a difficult time reconnecting with your greatness.

CHAPTER SIXTEEN

A New Way to Define Success in Business

Life-fulfilling work is never about the money—
when you feel true passion for something,
you instinctively find ways to nurture it.

—EILEEN FISHER

Our personal version of success is as unique to us as our fingerprints. And yet, far too many of us try to do things the way others do, hoping to have what they have—and then we wonder why we're not happy. We're chasing someone else's dreams without even realizing it. We're confusing our ego's longings with our soul's calling.

I think perhaps this was the hardest business lesson for me to learn. For years, I worked hard, did all the things I was told to do, and still didn't feel like I wasn't doing enough or that I had enough. I didn't know it yet, but I would find a match to my ideal version of success once I stopped looking around and comparing myself to others, and instead looked within.

One lazy Saturday afternoon, I had a sort of an epiphany that came to after me after a nap. I woke from a dreamlike state with a clear message in my head: "Who the fuck even cares about my success other than me? So why am I letting others, many of whom I don't even know, define it for me?"

That there is what my coach calls a BAM: a Bad Ass Moment. I realized how much power I was giving away to people who didn't even want it.

Bringing a fresh perspective to the table is tricky. The measure of business success has long been defined as the profits generated from it. Sadly, this gives little weight to the happiness of business owners, employees—or customers, for that matter. Those qualities are difficult to quantify, and most don't believe they have anything to do with the success of a business.

I've always found this sad. I've worked in places where my happiness wasn't valued over the billings I produced or the closings I handled. Happiness and how an individual feels haven't historically been considered in businesses. But I do believe this is changing. A few companies, like mine, and maybe like yours, are realizing you'll be much more successful if you nurture your employees, and not just take from them.

Metaphysical Wisdom

As a Business Alchemist, I've found that applying many of the lessons I've learned in my metaphysical studies have helped increase the financial abundance of a business, as well as the personal satisfaction of all involved. As I've said earlier, the idea that there is a separation of our true selves in work and at home is absurd. We are who we are, period! Going to work and leaving your soul behind so you can conform to a societal standard of how you should perform only causes strife and frustration, and can lead to depression.

We've all heard of people who just up and left a high-paying career to start their own business and follow their passion. I believe those people simply couldn't take the soul-sucking conformity they were boxed into and stepped out, even though they were likely scared, with the intent of living and working in alignment for something that is bigger than they.

I believe there's something magical available to all of us, and that it can be used to create a successful business in alignment with what our soul desires. That with that magic, we can harness the power of our thoughts, trust our intuition, and go for what we want, if we're clear on what that is.

Learning advertising and marketing, or anything else, is easy. In fact, you can hire someone to do that. The one thing you can't really outsource or delegate is you, and the special way you do your special thing. Your passion, your creativity, your authenticity, your enthusiasm, and your uniqueness are all key ingredients that will make your business successful. This is what I call your sparkle—it's different for you than it is for anyone else.

When I started out in business, I sought advice and

inspiration from other people who appeared to be successful—outwardly, at least. I did this through the material
I read and the workshops I attended, as well as with the
people I met at networking events and who I let person-
ally coach me. While many of the ideas they proscribed
appeared to have validity, I didn't find many of those ideas
comfortable or in alignment with my beliefs. Approaches
like cold calling, chasing people until they "buy or die,"
or pretending to be someone who I wasn't didn't suit me.

Funny, I'd started my business seeking freedom,
and found myself trapped in a business world that didn't
agree with my soul—and I wasn't alone. Over the years,
I've met many others with the same complaints who have
struggled in business because of limiting information
that doesn't feel like the right approach.

In the study of most metaphysical material, we
learn that our thoughts create things. I spoke to this
earlier in the book. We are powerful and have access
to an unlimited supply of creative energy, which some
call God, that will help us manifest anything we wish
for. When we tune into that creative energy, we are
guided to the inspired action that leads us to the people, resources, and ideas we need to fulfill our heart's
desires. Yet many of us spend more time looking for
outside validation or inspiration instead of listening to
our own inner wise women.

Our work is to affirm our heart's desires, to focus
clearly on our intent, believing as if the manifestations
are actually here, and then look for the right path to take,
via signs or intuition, to move in the direction of what we

desire. This is where visualization work and vision boards come in handy. This same creative energy is the master creator who created everything you see around you. Don't you think that that same energy could help you create a successful business in alignment with your higher purpose? Of course it can. Why swim upstream, trying to get a goal accomplished because that's what others tell us to do, when we could get in a boat and allow the stream to gently take us to our desired destination instead?

Our thoughts are pretty powerful, and it's those thoughts that got us where we are. If we want something different, we've got to be open to thinking differently. I have endless examples from my own life experience to demonstrate how I created exactly what I thought about. Some of those I've shared here in this book with you.

I bet you have many of your own. That's cool. I don't believe we came into the world at this time to be perfect, to have everything just so. We came here to learn, to have experiences, and to grow. Some of us simply take a little longer than others to learn. The way I see it, we're having different experiences. We're not doing it right or wrong. We're doing it our way.

Power Up Your Thoughts

Like many, I used to have a job that didn't allow me freedom or flexibility. That was exactly what I was looking for when I left, and it was my attention to it that helped me take the leap and go out on my own.

Rather than changing my thoughts after I launched my business, however, I kept thinking of freedom as something in the future, something I'd have to work hard to achieve. So that's exactly what I did; I created a business that didn't allow me any freedom either. Ironic, right?

What I believed, at the time, was that my worth or value came from the number of hours I put in. And, like many, I felt that I wasn't worthy of much more than a few dollars more per hour than I was earning at my last job. If I wanted to increase my income, I figured, I'd need to increase the number of hours I worked. With only twenty-four in a day, it didn't take long for frustration and burnout to set in. Talk about freedom buzz kill.

One day, I came across the work of Florence Scovel Shinn, who wrote *The Game of Life and How to Play It*. This brilliant author was a teacher in the early part of the last century who believed in the power of our thoughts. Thanks to her ideas, and to tuning into my inner wise woman, I started to see my business differently. While I wasn't making millions, I was making a nice living and providing a great service, employment for many, and flexibility for myself. Rather than be frustrated by a measure of success I wasn't in alignment with, I was now celebrating what I had accomplished and the impact my work was having.

I'd changed my focus from comparison with others or their ideas about success to something that was personal to me, and began affirming it daily. I was letting my brain catch up to what my heart knew to be true. In addition to manifesting many of these things I felt were important in my business, I also found I was a much happier person. I was listening to my intuition when making business decisions and not relying solely on so-called experts. What initially I found hard to believe was that I could intuitively know what I needed to do for myself and my business, and I didn't have to rely on outside experts as much. *Shazam!*

This doesn't mean I stopped reading books, watching videos, or attending workshops, and I haven't been without a coach to help me in many years. What it meant was that I didn't rely solely on outside advice. I now check in with my inner guidance before deciding to do something. This is exactly how I coach my clients—I share wisdom, they decide what feels right to them, and we go from there.

From Struggle to Success

Over the years, I've helped others shift their definition of success. By breaking free from the barriers they've created and tapping into their inner wisdom, they found or re-connected to their passion, came to believe in their dreams, and took action based on their intuition. Sometimes I have to pinch myself when I think about how simple this is and how this one lesson can transform struggling businesses (and their stressed-out owners) into a thriving, soulful enterprise.

My client Jane had struggled to find time for activities outside business. It had been many years since she'd had taken a full day off, let alone a real vacation. At the time we met she didn't like what she did, yet saw no end in sight due to financial obligations. A coach she was working with had told her to work hard, save up, and then take time off later. Jane wasn't happy with this, and it was showing.

I can't blame her. Who knows what tomorrow will bring? I always tell people there's more to life than business. Even for those who love what they do, spending time doing other things is equally important. After all, people on their deathbed never say they wished they'd worked another day. Instead, they wish they'd done more things they enjoyed, like spending time with family and friends, or pursuing something pleasurable. I believe that experiences outside of the work we do help nourish our body, mind, and soul, and provide us with creative inspiration we simply can't access when we're in the grind of things.

Over several meetings, Jane and I discovered that she was working from a place of limiting beliefs. While a part of her thought something better was possible, her actions didn't match up. Years of self-programming led Jane to believe that she couldn't take time off from her business—her clients were relying on her! She'd even said at several of our meetings that "no one else can do it the way I do."

Jane wanted to travel, spend time with her children and grandchildren, and improve her health, yet she wasn't allowing any of it to happen. Like me, she'd grown up with well-meaning parents who'd told us to "clean your room before you can go out and play," something she was still doing to the point of sheer exhaustion.

Together, Jane and I created a personal affirmation for her. She began to meditate, schedule time off, delegate some tasks, automate a few, and eliminate others. Jane even bought airline tickets far in advance for a trip to a foreign country, both making the commitment to go and affirming her belief that she was able to have both a business and a happy life.

As Jane and I continued to work together, she reported that when she took a few days off here, and there that her clients didn't miss her as much as she feared. Her excitement for freedom gave her an energetic boost, and she found she was able to get more done in less time than before.

There are thousands of business courses and books that wish us to believe that if we aren't good at something—accounting, sales, cold calling—all we have to do is read this, take that, do this, and we'll be "fixed." Here's the secret, my friend. You are perfect exactly as you are. You have within you everything you need to fulfill your soul's purpose. God created you in all your beautiful uniqueness to live the life you are living. There is nothing wrong with you, and there is nothing that needs fixing. Don't let anyone tell you otherwise.

That doesn't mean we can't learn something new. I have great curiosity, which I love to feed through books, audio programs, workshops, and seminars. But don't let your interest in a new skill take away from the real passion you have for helping others or being of service to a higher good through your business.

Maybe you think something like, say, cold calling, isn't a strength. You don't really want to do it, and yet you feel it's the way to build your business, so you enlist in a training course. Now you spend your time focusing on something you don't like to do and improving a skill you don't enjoy. Worse yet, you don't feel in alignment with how you'd like to run your business.

Ask me how I know this? It's because that was what I did for years, and it didn't work! Make better use of your time by focusing on what you like and what you want more of, and then attracting that into your life. Don't waste your time on things you're not interested in.

The power of aligned action might not be quantifiably measurable in a way the business world defines as successful. But metaphysical studies show countless examples of the benefits of focusing on what you *do* want, rather than what you *don't*. That doesn't mean ignoring things that aren't working. Instead, you're focusing on the change you *can* make, and taking action in alignment with what you'd truly like to feel in your life.

It's your individual belief, rather than society's, that will determine what takes place in your lives and your small business. None of us want a business where we work with people we don't enjoy and do things we don't like just to make a buck. I, for one, think that sounds like what most of us wanted to escape when we decided to start our own businesses.

It's your life. Live it in the way that makes you feel excited about the work you do.

Your Turn

How do you define success? What is your soul calling you to do that your ego may be blocking you from doing?

List four or five things that define success for you. Now, for each one, see if you can "flip" your definition of success to one that speaks to you in a way that will bring you closer to the way you really want to live your life and how you wish to feel in your work.

Epilogue

Thank you for being a part of this journey. It's been an adventure unlike any I ever dreamed up when I decided to embark on the path to entrepreneurship.

Don't believe for one moment that I have it all figured out. Even as I'm finishing this book, working on tweaks and rewrites with my editor, I'm thinking of new stories I wish I'd shared here. I am remembering lessons I've learned, and the many I want to learn, in this lifetime.

Just last week, I was to my client Bess, who was trying to figure something out. She's a numbers girl, and was struggling to make the numbers work to suit the situation she had. She'd run through several different scenarios, and none of them were working to solve this in a way she wanted. Her frustration was palpable.

I suggested that Bess take a break from the math and try something different for a few weeks. Rather than running new scenarios, I suggested she visualize how she wanted the situation to look and feel. I asked her to stop worrying about how it would happen, and instead spend five minutes every day visualizing how it would feel when this situation is resolved. I told her I kept hearing, "Enough with the math, now let in some magic."

Sometimes, we need a break and to let the magic do its thing. Sometimes we're just too close to the situation, and when we step back and let the Universe work its magic, solutions we never imagined come to us. Our work is to feel into it, to allow the solutions to come to us, and then take inspired action.

Other times, we just have to hold things together with duct tape. It might not be as pretty as we'd like, nor running as smoothly as we wish, but nonetheless, we're moving forward, and we're using this duct tape to hold it together while we focus on finding ways to improve it.

I want to leave you with a belief that I share with the Grand Ginger Princess: *Everything looks better with a little glitter on it*. Don't be afraid to sparkle and shine your light. We live in a beautiful and messy world. It's up to us to be the change we want to see in it. I believe that we can make the world a better place just by following our soul's calling and living the dreams we came here to live.

For the last few years, I've had the honor of working with many different small business owners who, like me, said yes to the entrepreneurial journey. Coaching them has been one of the most rewarding things I've ever done. I've cried with them, I've laughed with them, I've celebrated with them, and I've seen many find solutions to challenges that have allowed them to have Soul Crafted Success.

If there's a place where you're stuck, a challenge you're facing, or a solution you're seeking, please visit my website, www.MichelleSpalding.com, and pick up a copy of my audio program and workbook, *Soul Crafted Success*. While you're there, explore my other resources to help you create the life and business of your dreams.

Acknowledgments

To my family—thank you for inspiring me and encouraging me. And putting up with me when I locked you out of the office so I could write. I love you all.

To my soul sister Amy, thank you for your unwavering friendship on this journey—I look forward to many more marathon calls together and visits to the beach.

To my coach Regena, thank you for helping me see the gifts I have and their value in the world.

To Maggie, my editor, thank you for helping me give birth to another book.

And to the Grand Ginger Princess—thank you for choosing me to be your Gigi and for the fun times we have exploring, playing with fairies, and making art.

About the Author

Michelle Spalding is a multi-passionate entrepreneur who knew from a very young age she wanted to be a writer, teacher and businesswoman and was often found mowing lawns or babysitting in her teens.

Michelle started her first business in 2005, which  has steadily grown over the years. In 2015, she published her first book, *The Road from Contract to Close*, which led to many requests for coaching. Wanting to help others where she saw a real need, in late 2017, she launched the TC Academy to share all she could about being a TC and running a business.

Today, as a Business Alchemist she works with female entrepreneurs, helping them to transform obstacles allowing them to create the life and business of their soul is calling them to. She has an almost magic-like ability to find simple solutions to complicated issues and believes that women who know their value and do the work that inspires them to make the world a better place.

When she isn't working, you'll find her playing with Amelia, the Grand Ginger Princess, or snuggled up in her favorite chair reading a book.

Thank You

Thanks for reading—if you're If you'd like to receive Michelle's *Soul Crafted Success* workbook and MP3, please visit www.MichelleSpalding.com

For information on coaching, consulting and other resources please visit: MichelleSpalding.com.

Michelle is all over the web. You can get social with her at:
linkedin.com/in/michellespalding
twitter.com/mdspalding
instagram.com/MichelleSpalding
facebook.com/MichelleSpalding11

Made in the USA
Coppell, TX
21 April 2023

15896733R00121